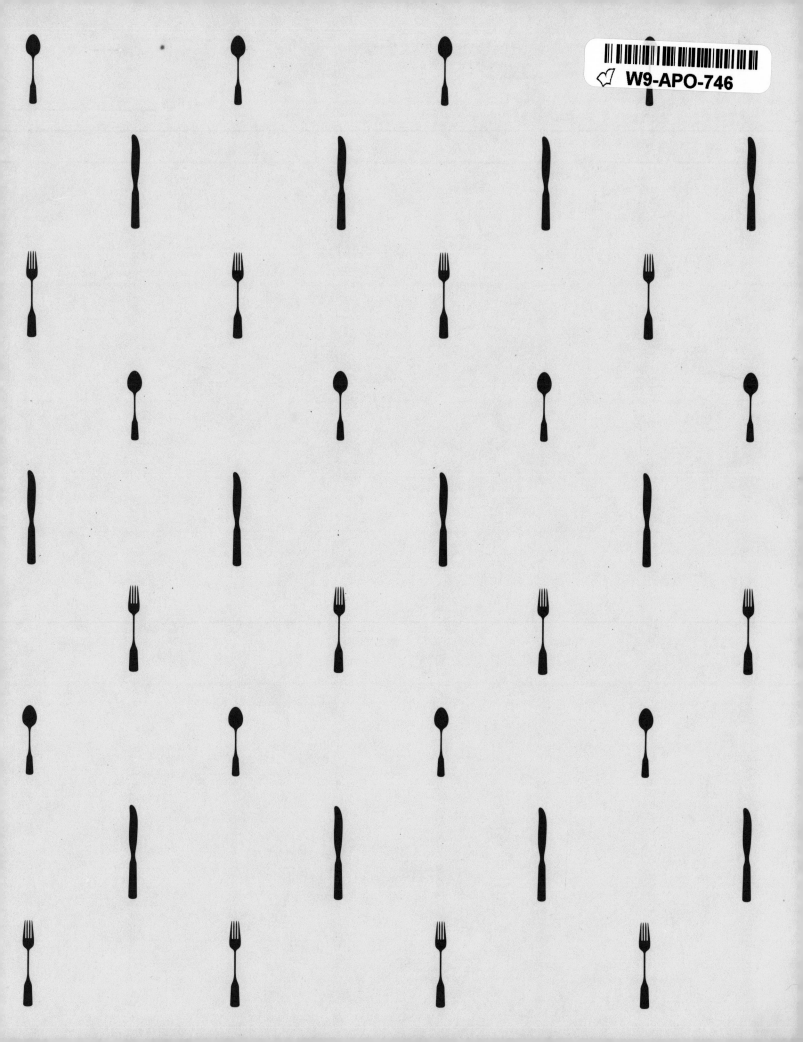

Fresh Ways
with Snacks & Party Fare

Time-Life Books Inc.
is a wholly owned subsidiary of
TIME INCORPORATED

FOUNDER: Henry R. Luce 1898-1967

Editor-in-Chief: Jason McManus
Chairman and Chief Executive Officer: J. Richard Munro
President and Chief Operating Officer: N. J. Nicholas, Jr.
Editorial Director: Ray Cave
Executive Vice President, Books: Kelso F. Sutton
Vice President, Books: George Artandi

COVER
Vivid colors and elegant shapes make this assortment of canapés (recipes, pages 50-53) the culinary height of any party. Low-fat toppings—such as fish mousse, asparagus tips, and breasts of chicken and duck—are set on bread bases and embellished with a shimmering layer of vegetable aspic.

TIME® LIFE BOOKS

TIME-LIFE BOOKS INC.

EDITOR: George Constable
Executive Editor: Ellen Phillips
Director of Design: Louis Klein
Director of Editorial Resources: Phyllis K. Wise
Editorial Board: Russell B. Adams, Jr., Dale M. Brown, Roberta Conlan, Thomas H. Flaherty, Lee Hassig, Donia Ann Steele, Rosalind Stubenberg, Henry Woodhead
Director of Photography and Research: John Conrad Weiser
Assistant Director of Editorial Resources: Elise Ritter Gibson

EUROPEAN EDITOR: Kit van Tulleken
Assistant European Editor: Gillian Moore
Design Director: Ed Skyner
Chief of Research: Vanessa Kramer
Chief Sub-Editor: Ilse Gray

PRESIDENT: Christopher T. Linen
Chief Operating Officer: John M. Fahey, Jr.
Senior Vice Presidents: Robert M. DeSena, James L. Mercer, Paul R. Stewart
Vice Presidents: Stephen L. Bair, Ralph J. Cuomo, Neal Goff, Stephen L. Goldstein, Juanita T. James, Hallett Johnson III, Carol Kaplan, Susan J. Maruyama, Robert H. Smith, Joseph J. Ward
Director of Production Services: Robert J. Passantino

Library of Congress Cataloging in Publication Data
Fresh ways with snacks & party fare / by the editors of Time-Life Books.
p.   cm. — (Healthy home cooking)
Includes index.
ISBN 0-8094-6037-8   ISBN 0-8094-6038-6 (lib. bdg.)
1. Snack foods.   2. Entertaining.
I. Time-Life Books.   II. Title: Fresh ways with snacks and party fare.   III. Series.
TX740.F673 1988   641.5'3—dc19   88-20014

For information on and a full description of any Time-Life Books series, please call 1-800-621-7026 or write:
Reader Information
Time-Life Customer Service
P.O. Box C-32068
Richmond, Virginia 23261-2068

Time-Life Books Inc. offers a wide range of fine recordings, including a *Rock 'n' Roll Era* series. For subscription information, call 1-800-621-7026 or write Time-Life Music, P.O. Box C-32068, Richmond, Virginia 23261-2068.

HEALTHY HOME COOKING

Editorial Staff for *Fresh Ways with Snacks & Party Fare:*

SERIES DIRECTOR: Jackie Matthews
Researcher: Susie Dawson
Designers: Lynne Brown, Mike Snell
Sub-Editor: Wendy Gibbons
Studio Stylist: Liz Hodgson
Studio Assistant: Rita Walters
Editorial Assistant: Eugénie Romer
Indexer: Myra Clark

Editorial Production for the series:
Chief: Maureen Kelly
Assistant: Samantha Hill
Editorial Department: Theresa John, Debra Lelliott

U.S. Edition:
Assistant Editor: Barbara Fairchild Quarmby
Copy Coordinator: Colette Stockum
Picture Coordinator: Betty H. Weatherley

Editorial Operations
Copy Chief: Diane Ullius
Production: Celia Beattie
Library: Louise D. Forstall

Correspondents: Elizabeth Kraemer-Singh (Bonn); Maria Vincenza Aloisi (Paris); Ann Natanson (Rome).

THE CONTRIBUTORS

PAT ALBUREY is a home economist with a wide experience in preparing foods for photography, teaching cooking, and creating recipes. She has written a number of cookbooks, and she was the studio consultant for the Time-Life Books series The Good Cook.

JOANNA BLYTHMAN is an amateur cook and recipe writer who owns a specialty food shop in Edinburgh, Scotland. She contributes articles on cooking to a number of newspapers and periodicals.

LISA CHERKASKY has worked as a chef at numerous restaurants in Washington, D.C., and in Madison, Wisconsin, including nationally known Le Pavillon and Le Lion d'Or. A graduate of The Culinary Institute of America at Hyde Park, New York, she has also taught classes in French cooking technique.

SILVIJA DAVIDSON studied at Leith's School of Food and Wine in London and specializes in the development of recipes from Latvia, as well as other international cuisines.

JANICE MURFITT trained as a home economist and has worked as an editor for *Family Circle* magazine. Her books include *Cheesecakes and Flans, Entertaining Friends,* and *Rice and Pasta.*

JEREMY ROUND, a former deputy editor of the *Good Food Guide,* is food correspondent for *The Independent* in London and the author of a book on Turkish regional cooking.

The following people also have contributed recipes to this volume: Alexandra Carlier, Graeme Gore-Rowe, Yvonne Hamlett, Carole Handslip, Antony Kwok, and Lyn Rutherford.

THE COOKS

The recipes in this book were prepared for photographing by Pat Alburey, Jacki Baxter, Allyson Birch, Jill Eggleton, Joanna Farrow, Anne Gains, Carole Handslip, Antony Kwok, Dolly Meers, Janice Murfitt, Lesley Sendall, and Michelle Thompson.

THE NUTRITION CONSULTANT

PATRICIA JUDD trained as a dietician and worked in hospital nutrition before returning to college to earn her M.Sc. and Ph.D. degrees. She has since lectured in Nutrition and Dietetics at London University.

Nutritional analyses for *Fresh Ways with Snacks & Party Fare* were derived from McCance and Widdowson's *The Composition of Food* by A. A. Paul and D. A. T. Southgate, and other current data.

Other Publications:

THE TIME-LIFE GARDENER'S GUIDE
MYSTERIES OF THE UNKNOWN
TIME FRAME
FIX IT YOURSELF
FITNESS, HEALTH & NUTRITION
SUCCESSFUL PARENTING
UNDERSTANDING COMPUTERS
LIBRARY OF NATIONS
THE ENCHANTED WORLD
THE KODAK LIBRARY OF CREATIVE PHOTOGRAPHY
GREAT MEALS IN MINUTES
THE CIVIL WAR
PLANET EARTH
COLLECTOR'S LIBRARY OF THE CIVIL WAR
THE EPIC OF FLIGHT
THE GOOD COOK
WORLD WAR II
HOME REPAIR AND IMPROVEMENT
THE OLD WEST

This volume is one of a series of illustrated cookbooks that emphasize the preparation of healthful dishes for today's weight-conscious, nutrition-minded eaters.

Fresh Ways with Snacks & Party Fare

BY

THE EDITORS OF TIME-LIFE BOOKS

TIME-LIFE BOOKS / ALEXANDRIA, VIRGINIA

Contents

Crudités on Skewers with Spiced Peanut Dip

Green-Jacket Rock Shrimp

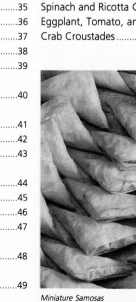

Miniature Samosas

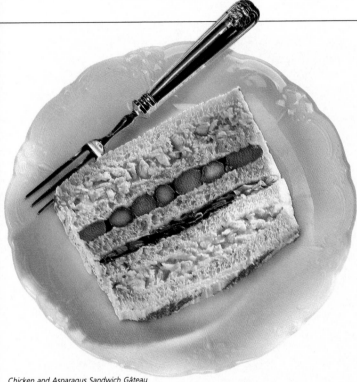

Chicken and Asparagus Sandwich Gâteau

Goat Cheese on Toast

Baked Oysters

Hospitable Fare

Eating between meals, or relying on a snack to take the place of one, may come high on the list of nutritional sins. But occasionally, most of us succumb to temptation or necessity. Visiting friends on the spur of the moment or attending a special celebration, we are hard pressed to refuse the refreshments offered: The sharing of food is, after all, the heart and soul of hospitality. Coming home after an evening out, a full-scale dinner is often out of the question; instead, we content ourselves with a snack.

But sociable or casual eating does not need to be self-destructive. Food consumed between meals, or instead of them, can be light, wholesome, high in nutrients, and low in those banes of the contemporary diet: saturated fats, sugar, and excess salt. This volume presents a new approach to formal and informal entertaining that is a world away from the usual assortment of fat-laden, oversalted chips and nuts, thick mayonnaise dips, and stodgy, calorie-laden canapés. It provides a repertoire of food for all occasions, formal or informal, large or small, planned weeks in advance or conjured up as an impromptu treat.

The volume is divided into four chapters. The first two offer ideas for parties: Chapter 1 concentrates on cold party food, Chapter 2 on hot. Informal snacks, including sandwiches, are covered in the third chapter, while the final section of the book presents recipes uniquely suited to microwave cooking. All 126 recipes have been devised in accordance with contemporary nutritional thinking, emphasizing the use of fresh, natural ingredients, with minimal reliance on saturated fats and salt, and an avoidance, wherever possible, of processed foods.

Butter is used in small quantities, or replaced by polyunsaturated oils where appropriate, and low-fat yogurt substitutes for cream. Meat is scrupulously trimmed of fat; poultry is likewise freed of fat and skin. Much use is made of fresh vegetables and fruit; herbs and spices serve as natural sources of flavor; excessively rich sauces are abandoned in favor of light dressings and aromatic marinades.

Moderation, rather than rigid abstinence, is the governing principle. A certain amount of fat, for instance, is necessary to keep the human body in good working order and to help transform the foods we eat into usable energy. But too much fat—particularly the saturated fats found in fatty meats and dairy products—is now generally believed to contribute to heart disease, obesity, digestive disorders, and according to recent research, to the development of certain cancers.

Ironically, the snacks that most people find hardest to resist, and easiest to consume far too many of, are those that are highest in fat content: savory tidbits such as potato chips, corn chips, and other items that derive their golden color and eminently satisfying crunch from immersion in a pot of bubbling fat. Fortunately, there are other ways to achieve a pleasurably crunchy texture. Broiling foods instead of deep-frying, or sautéing them in a small amount of oil—such as sunflower or safflower—that is high in polyunsaturated fats, produces excellent results. Bite-size savory crackers made from low-fat dough flavored with Parmesan cheese, sesame seeds, or crushed garlic, are lighter and less cloying than the ubiquitous party snacks sold commercially in cans or packets; lightly toasted chickpeas make a pleasant and healthful change from greasy salted nuts.

Salt, too, has been the subject of concern and controversy. Salt occurs naturally in many foods; it is a traditional and effective preservative, and a certain amount of salt is essential for good health. Yet practically everyone who eats a typical Western diet, and consumes any quantity of processed food, is taking in salt far in excess of his or her bodily needs. People with blood-pressure problems, in particular, are often warned by their doctors to cut down on salt or cut it out altogether. But an inspired use of other flavorings can render salt on snacks superfluous. Popcorn, for instance, gains savor from a spicy tomato coating or from curry spices, while an easy recipe for homemade pretzels coats the twists in herbs instead of salt.

Favorites from around the world

Cuisines from many different nations lend fresh inspiration. From Spain comes a substantial omelet of peppers and potatoes that uses only half an egg per serving. India contributes samosas and kofta—pastry triangles enclosing a spicy filling and aromatic meatballs made with ground chicken. Provence supplies a vinaigrette-dressed salad in a sandwich, indispensable for picnics at the beach. Delicacies with a Middle Eastern influence range from chickpea and yogurt dip to the little cigar-shaped phyllo pastries known as *sigara borek*. Peru provides its own exotic, high-protein favorite—skewered morsels of chili-spiced beef heart that will tempt even the most unadventurous of meat eaters. From China, which has elevated the between-meals snack into a national pastime, come sesame shrimp toasts—made here without resorting to deep-fat frying—and seafood won tons, filled in this instance with a very European combination of fresh and smoked salmon. Japanese sushi, the elegant parcels of fresh fish, rice, and seaweed, are presented along with some cosmopolitan variations on the theme: ruby-red radicchio leaves as wrappers, or slivers of red pepper, avocado, and olives augmenting the traditional seafood filling.

Hand-held delicacies

At any party where guests are intended to move around and mingle, perilous balancing acts with glasses, plates, and eating

The Key to Better Eating

Healthy Home Cooking addresses the concerns of today's weight-conscious, health-minded cooks with recipes that take into account guidelines set by nutritionists. The secret of eating well, of course, has to do with maintaining a balance of foods in the diet; most of us consume too much sugar and salt, too much fat, too many calories, and more protein than we need. In planning a snack, the recipes should be used thoughtfully, in the context of a day's eating. To make the choice easier, this book presents an analysis of nutrients either in a single snack serving, as in the breakdown on the right, or per item. When a dish includes a sauce or dip, the per-item analysis includes a proportion of the sauce. The cook should also bear in mind that moderation, as in all things, is a good policy to follow.

Interpreting the chart

The chart at right shows the National Research Council's Recommended Dietary Allowances of calories and protein for healthy men, women, and children, along with the council's recommendations for the "safe and adequate" intake of sodium. Although the council has not established recommendations for either cholesterol or fat, the chart includes what the National Institutes of Health and the American Heart Association consider the daily maximum amounts for healthy members of the population. The Heart Association, among other groups, has pointed out that Americans derive about 40 percent of their calories from fat; this, it believes, should be cut to less than 30 percent.

The volumes in the Healthy Home Cooking series do not purport to be diet books, nor do they focus on health foods. Rather, they express a common-sense approach to cooking that uses salt, sugar, cream, butter, and oil in moderation while employing other ingredients that also provide flavor and satisfaction. Herbs, spices, aromatic vegetables, fruit, and vinegars are all used to achieve this end.

Calories **250**
Protein **23g.**
Cholesterol **70mg.**
Total fat **11g.**
Saturated fat **3g.**
Sodium **185mg.**

The recipes make few unusual demands. Naturally, they call for fresh ingredients, offering substitutes when these are unavailable. (The substitute is not calculated in the nutrient analysis, however.) Most of the ingredients can be found in any well-stocked supermarket; the exceptions can be bought in specialty or ethnic shops.

In Healthy Home Cooking's test kitchens, heavy-bottomed pots and pans are used to guard against foods burning and sticking whenever a small amount of oil is used; non-stick pans are utilized as well. Both safflower oil and virgin olive oil are favored for sautéing. Safflower oil was chosen because it is the most highly polyunsaturated vegetable fat available in supermarkets, and polyunsaturated fats reduce blood cholesterol; if unobtainable, use sunflower oil, also high in polyunsaturated fats. Virgin olive oil is used because it has a fine fruity flavor lacking in the lesser grade known as "pure." In addition, it is—like all olive oil—high in mono-unsaturated fats, which are thought not to increase blood cholesterol. Virgin olive and safflower oils can be combined, with olive oil contributing its fruitiness to the safflower oil. When virgin olive oil is unavailable, "pure" may be substituted.

About cooking times

To help the cook plan ahead effectively, Healthy Home Cooking takes time into account in all of its recipes. While recognizing that everyone cooks at a different speed, and that stoves and ovens differ in temperatures, the series provides approximate "working" and "total" times for every dish. Working time denotes the minutes actively spent on preparation; total time includes unattended cooking time, as well as any other time devoted to marinating, chilling, or soaking various ingredients. Since the recipes emphasize fresh foods, they may take a little longer to prepare than quick and easy dishes that call for canned or packaged products, but the payoff in flavor and often in nutrition should compensate for the extra time involved.

Recommended Dietary Guidelines

		Average Daily Intake		Maximum Daily Intake			
		CALORIES	PROTEIN grams	CHOLESTEROL milligrams	TOTAL FAT grams	SATURATED FAT grams	SODIUM milligrams
Children	7-10	2400	22	240	80	27	1800
Females	11-14	2200	37	220	73	24	2700
	15-18	2100	44	210	70	23	2700
	19-22	2100	44	300	70	23	3300
	23-50	2000	44	300	67	22	3300
	51-75	1800	44	300	60	20	3300
Males	11-14	2700	36	270	90	30	2700
	15-18	2800	56	280	93	31	2700
	19-22	2900	56	300	97	32	3300
	23-50	2700	56	300	90	30	3300
	51-75	2400	56	300	80	27	3300

utensils are best avoided. The ideal refreshments are those that can be eaten by hand. Tidbits such as small sandwiches or bread pinwheels, stuffed cherry tomatoes or mushroom caps, cheese balls rolled in herbs and spices, fresh dates filled with smoked beef and mozzarella, are all easy to eat neatly with the fingers, as are morsels of seafood, such as butterfly shrimp. Fresh vegetables make excellent scoops for dips, or bases for other ingredients: A crisp array of cauliflower sticks, sweet-pepper strips, and other crudités accompanies a hot tomato dip; endive leaves and snow peas envelop colorful purées of peas and carrots. Other unusual containers include anise-flavored crepes formed into fans for easy dipping, or pancakes molded and baked into crisp cups to receive a filling of green peas in a creamy mustard sauce.

Some foods, by their very shape and structure, lend themselves naturally to being eaten with the fingers. Chicken wings or glazed drumsticks, for instance, or mussels topped with tomato and fennel and served on the half shell, are easy to handle. With the help of small skewers or cocktail sticks, other items can be conveniently speared on their own or assembled as brochettes: Multicolored, mushroom-filled tortellini, miniature kabobs of pork and fennel or turkey and cranberries, cubes of monkfish wrapped in ham, and baby baked potatoes in a coating of Parmesan cheese, are only a few of countless possibilities.

Showpieces for grand occasions

Many of the recipes in this book can be prepared in minutes. But speedy preparation is not always a priority. For an enthusiastic cook, the time spent in the kitchen before a large party or special celebration is part and parcel of the pleasure the event provides. These are the occasions when culinary artistry can flower, indeed run rampant. Yet it is possible to create a veritable feast without sending the guests' salt or saturated-fat consumption soaring. Jewel-like canapés of asparagus, shrimp, and haddock, of carefully trimmed chicken breast or duck, all shimmering in coats of aspic, are rich in flavor only. Shells of chou-puff dough—made lighter by using fewer eggs than most recipes call for—can be studded with pine nuts for an intriguing variation in texture and combined with a delicately flavored mushroom filling; croustade cases are crisped in the oven with only the slightest brushing of oil, to hold scallops in a tarragon-lemon sauce, or a vibrant mixture of eggplant, tomato, and crab. Some presentations, such as a magnificent, multilayered chicken and asparagus sandwich gâteau, demand a fair amount of care; however, they amply repay these efforts by the admiration they elicit at serving time.

If you are tempted to try a new and relatively complicated recipe for a special event, allow yourself, if possible, the luxury of a trial run, and let friends or family reap the benefits of this culinary dress rehearsal.

A matter of logistics

Even the most elaborate creations are simplified by a little forward planning. Yeast dough for pizzas and calzone, pastry for quiches and tartlets, fresh pasta dough, and pancake batters can all be made ahead of time and stored in the refrigerator until needed; many sauces, dips, and marinades will even improve in flavor if prepared a day or so in advance. When you are organizing a party, save eleventh-hour panics in the kitchen by devising a menu that includes only one or two items that require last-minute attention.

If you are catering for large numbers, it is best to avoid the temptation of offering too vast an array of different dishes, confusing the eye and palate, and detracting from the appreciation each delicacy deserves. Limit the number of elements, and make whatever you choose in multiple batches: Doubling or tripling the quantities in a recipe does not necessarily double or triple the time required to produce it. For ease of serving, aim for a mixture of hot and cold items, including some that will not suffer if they are set out well before your guests arrive, or that can be held in a low oven without detriment. And, just as you would for an ordinary dinner party, compose a menu that is well balanced in flavors, textures, and appearance: A spread with too many items of the same color, or accompanied by similar sauces, may be overwhelming and disappointing at the same time. The best results will be achieved by an imaginative mix of dishes, featuring different main ingredients, that complement each other rather than compete for attention. And, since most people now number at least one vegetarian among their acquaintances, make sure all your guests enjoy the party by including a selection of snacks made without meat or fish.

No such advance planning is necessary, or possible, for spur-of-the-moment treats for family members or unexpected guests. Instead, take the pressure off the cook by enlisting the rest of the company as helpers to slice bread, make toast, chop herbs, or assemble garnishes. With a few additional willing hands in the kitchen, even the most elaborate snack can be put together in a matter of minutes, producing results that are far more delicious and healthful, and infinitely more interesting than anything available in the oversalted, fat-laden world of so-called fast food.

Bread and Crackers for Snacks

Bread is an integral part of many snacks, from substantial stuffed loaves to dainty finger sandwiches and, most delicate of all, the bite-size canapé. The character of such snacks depends not only on the texture and flavor of the bread but on the way it is sliced, shaped, filled, or garnished.

The most versatile bread is the firm, close-grained white bread *(recipe, right)*. It can be sliced to any thickness; it toasts well; and when the slices are rolled out, they can be used for pinwheel sandwiches or shaped into croustades. Whole-wheat bread *(recipe, far right)* has a more crumbly texture, making it unsuitable for molding or for canapés but ideal for sandwiches.

The distinctive nutty flavor of dark rye breads and pumpernickel makes them good choices for strongly flavored foods such as smoked meats and fish. Their firm, even texture, which does not easily absorb moisture from fillings, also makes them good foundations for canapés and open sandwiches.

French loaves, or baguettes, can be split lengthwise and filled, or cut into small rounds and spread with a topping. And Middle Eastern pita bread can be halved and stuffed with anything from stir-fried vegetables and meats to salads and fruit. Toasted bread or crackers can be used to accompany dips and pâtés.

Bread that is slightly stale—about a day old—is easier to slice and shape than a fresh crumbly loaf. For best results, slice the bread with a sharp, long-bladed serrated knife. Alternatively, ask your baker to slice the bread by machine; this will ensure even slices of the required thickness.

Leftovers can be processed into fine crumbs and either frozen, or dried in a cool, airy place for two or three days; they may then be stored in an airtight container for up to three weeks. Larger pieces may be cut into croutons and frozen until needed.

White Sandwich Bread

Makes 1 large loaf
Working time: about 30 minutes
Total time: about 3 hours (includes proofing)

1 envelope (¼ oz.) active dry yeast
6 cups unbleached all-purpose flour
2 tsp. salt
2 tbsp. polyunsaturated margarine

Per whole loaf:
Calories **2,850**
Protein **75g.**
Cholesterol **0mg.**
Total fat **33g.**
Saturated fat **7g.**
Sodium **2,600mg.**

Add the yeast to 2 cups of tepid water and stir with a fork until the yeast has completely dissolved; then let the yeast mixture stand for 10 minutes. Meanwhile, sift the flour and salt into a large mixing bowl, and rub in the margarine.

Make a well in the center of the flour. Pour the yeast liquid into the well, then mix it together by hand to form a dough that is firm yet slightly sticky. Transfer the dough to a lightly floured surface, and knead well until the dough becomes very smooth and elastic—10 to 15 minutes. (Avoid adding too much flour as you knead: This will make the dough dry. As the dough is kneaded, it will become firmer and less sticky.) Alternatively, the dough may be mixed with a dough hook, or in a food processor with a special blade for mixing dough. (Check the manufacturer's instructions for the weight of dough your machine can mix at one time.)

Shape the kneaded dough into a ball and place it in a clean, lightly floured, mixing bowl. Cover the bowl with plastic wrap. Leave the bowl in a warm place until the dough has risen to double its original size—45 minutes to one hour. It should spring back when pressed with a lightly floured finger.

Transfer the risen dough to a very lightly floured work surface, and punch it back to its original size by firmly pounding it with clenched fists to expel the air bubbles. Reknead until the dough is smooth—two to three minutes.

Grease a pan that is 9½ by 5½ by 3 inches. Shape the dough into an oblong large enough to fit into the bottom of the pan. Place the dough in the pan, pressing it firmly into the corners, and loosely cover the pan with plastic wrap. Leave the pan in a warm place until the dough rises to the top of the loaf pan—30 to 45 minutes.

In the meantime, preheat the oven to 450° F. Remove the plastic wrap from the risen loaf, then bake the loaf until it is golden brown and has shrunk away from the sides of the pan—35 to 40 minutes. When it is turned out of the pan, tap the base of the loaf lightly with your knuckles; it should sound hollow. Place the loaf of bread on a wire rack to cool.

Whole-Wheat Sandwich Bread

Makes 1 large loaf
Working time: about 30 minutes
Total time: about 3 hours (includes proofing)

2 envelopes (½ oz.) active dry yeast
6 cups whole-wheat flour
1 tbsp. dark brown sugar
2 tsp. salt
4 tbsp. polyunsaturated margarine

Per whole loaf:
Calories **2,900**
Protein **103g.**
Cholesterol **0mg.**
Total fat **64g.**
Saturated fat **14g.**
Sodium **2,840mg.**

Make and bake the bread as directed for the white bread *(recipe, above)*, adding the brown sugar to the sifted flour and salt.

Whole-Wheat Pitas

Makes 16 pitas
Working time: about 40 minutes
Total time: about 2 hours and 15 minutes
(includes proofing)

4 cups whole-wheat flour
2 cups bread flour
2 tsp. salt
2 envelopes (½ oz.) active dry yeast
2 tbsp. virgin olive oil

Per pita:
Calories **170**
Protein **6g.**
Cholesterol **0mg.**
Total fat **3g.**
Saturated fat **trace**
Sodium **150mg.**

Make and proof the dough as for the white bread at left, adding the olive oil at the same time as the yeast liquid. Punch down the risen dough, then knead until smooth. Divide the dough into 16 pieces and shape each one into a ball. Cover the balls with plastic wrap.

Taking one ball at a time, roll the dough out to an oval shape about 7 inches long, then place it on a floured cloth. Cover the shaped pitas with a clean cloth, and leave them in a warm place for approximately 20 minutes to rise slightly. Meanwhile, preheat the oven to its highest setting.

Lightly oil several baking sheets and heat them in the oven for 10 minutes. Immediately, place the pitas on the hot baking sheets and bake them until they have puffed up—about 10 minutes. Transfer the pita bread to wire racks to cool.

Water Biscuits

Makes about 36 biscuits
Working time: about 20 minutes
Total time: about 35 minutes

2 cups unbleached all-purpose flour
½ tsp. salt
1½ tsp. baking powder
4 tbsp. polyunsaturated margarine

Per biscuit:
Calories **35**
Protein **1g.**
Cholesterol **0mg.**
Total fat **2g.**
Saturated fat **trace**
Sodium **50mg.**

Preheat the oven to 375° F. Grease several baking sheets. Sift the flour, salt, and baking powder into a mixing bowl. Rub the margarine into the flour until the mixture resembles fine breadcrumbs, then make a well in the center. Add 5 to 6 tablespoons of water and mix, using a wooden spoon, to make a firm dough.

Knead the dough on a lightly floured surface until smooth, then roll it out until it is almost paper thin. Prick the dough all over with a fork. Using a 3-inch plain round cutter, cut out rounds from the dough and place them on the baking sheets. Reknead and reroll the trimmings, then cut out more rounds; continue until the dough is used up.

Bake the biscuits until they are just lightly browned—10 to 15 minutes. Transfer them to wire racks to cool.

EDITOR'S NOTE: *To make herb-flavored biscuits, add 2 teaspoons of mixed dried herbs to the flour. Sesame seeds or poppy seeds may be sprinkled over the rolled-out dough and lightly rolled into the dough before the biscuits are cut out. The biscuits may be stored for up to one week in an airtight container.*

Melba Toast

Makes about 40 pieces
Working time: about 10 minutes
Total time: about 1 hour

½ large or 1 small loaf white bread, three to four days old

Per piece:
Calories **35**
Protein **1g.**
Cholesterol **0mg.**
Total fat **2g.**
Saturated fat **trace**
Sodium **50mg.**

Preheat the oven to 325° F. Cut the crusts off the bread, then slice the loaf as thin as possible. Cut each slice in half diagonally to make two triangles. Place the triangles on baking sheets in single layers.

Bake in the oven until the bread curls and becomes a very pale golden-brown, crisp toast—about 50 minutes. Spread the toasts out in a single layer on a wire rack to cool.

Serve the toasts cold or warmed through in a 350° F. oven for 5 to 10 minutes.

EDITOR'S NOTE: *Melba toast can be stored in an airtight container for up to two weeks.*

Chive and Oatmeal Crackers

Makes about 40 crackers
Working time: about 20 minutes
Total time: about 45 minutes

1 cup rolled oats, finely ground
1 cup unbleached all-purpose flour
1 tsp. baking powder
¼ tsp. salt
1 tbsp. finely chopped fresh chives
6 tbsp. polyunsaturated margarine

Per cracker:
Calories **40**
Protein **1g.**
Cholesterol **0mg.**
Total fat **2g.**
Saturated fat **trace**
Sodium **40mg.**

Preheat the oven to 350° F. Grease several baking sheets. Put the oats, flour, baking powder, salt, and chives into a bowl, and mix. Rub in the margarine until the mixture resembles breadcrumbs, then make a well in the center. Add 3 tablespoons of boiling water and mix, using a wooden spoon, to make a firm dough.

Knead the dough on a lightly floured surface until smooth, then roll it out to about ⅛ inch thick. Using a 2-inch plain round cutter, cut out rounds from the dough and place them on the baking sheets. Reknead and reroll the trimmings, then cut out more rounds; continue until the dough is used up.

Bake the crackers until they are cooked through and very lightly browned—20 to 25 minutes. Transfer to wire racks to cool.

EDITOR'S NOTE: *The crackers may be stored for up to one week in an airtight container.*

1 *Vegetable strips and shreds of lemon zest lie on a bed of sushi rice and dried seaweed ready to be rolled and sliced into eye-catching sushi (recipe, page 26).*

Cold Party Treats

Set out to greet the guests on their arrival, cold snacks are perhaps the partygiver's staunchest allies. Whether a plate of simple pretzels *(page 15)* or a collation of exotic sushi *(left)*, they can all be prepared in advance and arranged to make an attractive display.

Alongside some intriguing newcomers such as labne cocktail balls *(page 24)*—savory mouthfuls molded from strained yogurt—the recipes in this chapter include many familiar offerings, but they are contrived here with a lighter, more healthful touch. Stuffed eggs *(page 22)*, for example, are filled with a low-fat mixture of chive-flecked ricotta cheese in place of the usual dollops of mayonnaise. Cheese straws—normally made from high-fat puff pastry—are produced from a more wholesome dough that is low in fat and enriched with rolled oats *(page 16)*. And the chickpea dip on page 20, inspired by the Middle Eastern snack *hummus,* derives its creamy texture from yogurt rather than the traditional olive oil.

Many of the dishes in this chapter can be made well ahead of time, thus easing your final work load. The various savory appetizers, for instance, can be baked up to three days beforehand and, once cool, stored in airtight containers. Dips and sauces can be prepared a day or two ahead and kept covered with plastic wrap in the refrigerator until needed. Other offerings should be made on the day of the party. Those containing vegetables, such as the crudités on skewers *(page 19)*, should be assembled as late in the day as possible to ensure that they retain their fresh appearance and flavor. And the caviar canapés on page 25 must be put together at the last minute lest their bread bases, unprotected with butter or margarine, become soggy.

The most time-consuming but eye-catching party dishes are the aspic-coated canapés on pages 50 to 53, and these require careful planning. The vegetable aspic that gives them their gleaming coat can be made a couple of days before it is needed, and the main ingredients, such as duck or chicken breast, can be trimmed and prepared, tightly covered with plastic wrap, and refrigerated the day before the party. The final assembly must be completed about 20 minutes before serving: late enough to ensure that the decorative garnishes look fresh and bright, but early enough to allow the aspic to set in the refrigerator.

Cocktail Croutons

Makes about 200 croutons
Working time: about 30 minutes
Total time: about 45 minutes

Per 5 croutons:
Calories **40**
Protein **1g.**
Cholesterol **4mg.**
Total fat **2g.**
Saturated fat **1g.**
Sodium **4mg.**

12 thin slices day-old whole-wheat bread, about 5 by 4 inches each
4 tbsp. unsalted butter
1 tbsp. Dijon mustard
2 garlic cloves, crushed
2 tbsp. finely chopped parsley
¼ tsp. salt
⅛ tsp. cayenne pepper
1 oz. Parmesan cheese, finely grated (about ¼ cup)

Preheat the oven to 425° F.

Grease several baking sheets, and then remove the crusts from the bread. Put the butter into a bowl with the mustard, garlic, parsley, salt, and cayenne pepper. Beat together until the mixture is very soft and creamy.

Spread both sides of each slice of bread with the savory butter. Sprinkle one side of each slice of bread with the Parmesan cheese, then cut the slices into about 18 small triangles, as shown here, or into squares or oblongs.

Put the bread shapes on the baking sheets, and cook them in the oven until they are crisp and golden brown—10 to 15 minutes. Serve warm or cold.

Miniature Savory Puffs

Makes about 350 puffs
Working time: about 40 minutes
Total time: about 1 hour

Per 5 puffs:
Calories **65**
Protein **1g.**
Cholesterol **25mg.**
Total fat **4g.**
Saturated fat **2g.**
Sodium **65mg.**

6 tbsp. polyunsaturated margarine
¼ tsp. salt
1 cup unbleached all-purpose flour
2 eggs
1 egg white
½ cup finely grated Parmesan cheese
1 garlic clove, crushed
2 tbsp. finely cut fresh chives
1 tbsp. mixed dried herbs

Preheat the oven to 425° F.

Line several baking sheets with parchment paper. Have ready three pastry bags, each bag fitted with a ½-inch tip.

Put the margarine and salt into a saucepan with 1 cup of cold water, and heat on medium low until the margarine melts, then bring to a boil. Remove the pan from the heat and add the flour, stirring quickly with a wooden spoon at the same time. Return the pan to medium heat and stir for a few seconds, until the mixture forms a ball. Remove from the heat.

Add the eggs and the egg white one at a time to the flour and water paste, beating vigorously between each addition with a wooden spoon or a hand-held electric mixer.

Beat the Parmesan and garlic into the chou paste. Put one-third of the mixture into a pastry bag. Put another third of the mixture into a small bowl and beat in the chives, then spoon into another pastry bag. Beat the mixed herbs into the remaining chou paste, and spoon into the third pastry bag.

Pipe the chou paste onto the lined baking sheets in small mounds about ½ inch in diameter, spaced evenly apart. Bake in the oven until the choux are well risen, golden brown, and crisp—20 to 25 minutes. Remove the puffs from the baking sheets immediately and transfer to wire racks to cool. Serve the puffs within a couple of hours.

EDITOR'S NOTE: *The piped pastry may be stored for up to two hours in the refrigerator before baking. Alternatively, pipe the choux onto foil-lined trays and freeze. Then lift off the foil, stack, wrap, and store in the freezer. When necessary, place each foil sheet on a baking sheet and bake.*

Herb Pretzels

Makes about 40 pretzels
Working time: about 45 minutes
Total time: about 1 hour

Per 5 pretzels:
Calories **185**
Protein **5g.**
Cholesterol **35mg.**
Total fat **11g.**
Saturated fat **3g.**
Sodium **205mg.**

1 cup unbleached all-purpose flour
6 tbsp. whole-wheat flour
¼ tsp. salt
½ tsp. baking powder
1 tsp. mixed dried herbs
6 tbsp. polyunsaturated margarine
1 small egg, beaten
¼ cup finely grated Parmesan cheese

Preheat the oven to 400° F. Grease several baking sheets.

Sift the all-purpose and whole-wheat flour, salt, and baking powder into a mixing bowl, adding any bran left in the sieve. Mix in the herbs, then rub in the margarine until the mixture resembles fine breadcrumbs. Make a well in the center of the flour. Pour 5 tablespoons of boiling water into the well, then mix with a wooden spoon to form a soft dough. Knead the dough on a very lightly floured surface to smooth.

Divide the dough into about 40 small pieces. Take one piece of dough and roll it out with your hands into a thin strand, about 12 inches long.

Form a pretzel by shaping the strand into a curve, with its ends toward you. Cross the ends over, then take their points up to the center of the curve and press them firmly in position. Place the pretzel on a baking sheet. Shape the remaining pieces of dough in the same way.

Brush the pretzels lightly with the beaten egg, then sprinkle with the Parmesan cheese. Bake the pretzels in the oven until they are lightly browned—about 15 minutes. Carefully transfer the pretzels to a wire rack to cool.

EDITOR'S NOTE: *The pretzels may be stored in an airtight container for up to two days.*

Savory Nibbles

Makes about 250 nibbles
Working time: about 30 minutes
Total time: about 40 minutes

Per 5 nibbles:
Calories **85**
Protein **2g.**
Cholesterol **20mg.**
Total fat **6g.**
Saturated fat **2g.**
Sodium **120mg.**

1½ cups unbleached all-purpose flour
½ tsp. salt
½ tsp. baking powder
6 tbsp. polyunsaturated margarine
3 oz. Cheddar cheese, finely grated (about ¾ cup)
1 egg, lightly beaten
1 tsp. curry powder
1 garlic clove
2 tbsp. finely chopped parsley

Preheat the oven to 400° F.

Grease several baking sheets.

Sift the flour, half of the salt, and the baking powder into a mixing bowl. Rub the margarine into the flour until the mixture resembles fine breadcrumbs. Mix in the cheese. Add the egg and mix together with a wooden spoon to form a soft dough.

Gently knead the dough on a lightly floured surface until smooth, then roll out to an oblong approximately 12 by 18 inches. Using a fluted pastry wheel, cut the dough into long, thin strips, about ¾ inch wide. Cut across the strips to make diamonds, oblongs, or squares. Place the tiny crackers on the baking sheets and bake in the oven until they are golden brown—8 to 10 minutes. Transfer the crackers to wire racks to cool. Immediately, sift the curry powder over half of the crackers.

Put the garlic into a small mortar with the remaining salt and crush with a pestle until creamy. Mix in the parsley. When the plain crackers are cool, put them into a large bowl, add the garlic mixture, and mix very gently until the crackers are evenly coated. Serve the crackers in separate bowls.

Oatmeal Cheese Straws

Makes about 100 straws
Working (and total) time: about 1 hour

Per 5 straws:
Calories **65**
Protein **2g.**
Cholesterol **20mg.**
Total fat **5g.**
Saturated fat **2g.**
Sodium **90mg.**

½ cup rolled oats
½ cup unbleached all-purpose flour
½ tsp. baking powder
¼ tsp. salt
½ tsp. dry mustard
¼ tsp. cayenne pepper
4 tbsp. polyunsaturated margarine
2 oz. Cheddar cheese, finely grated (about ½ cup)
1 oz. Parmesan cheese, finely grated (about ¼ cup)
1 egg, beaten
2 tsp. skim milk

Preheat the oven to 400° F.

Grease several baking sheets.

Finely grind the rolled oats in a food processor, blender, or electric grinder. Sift the flour, baking powder, salt, mustard, and cayenne pepper into a mixing bowl. Mix in the oats, then rub in the margarine until the mixture resembles fine breadcrumbs. Mix in the Cheddar cheese and half of the Parmesan cheese; add the egg and mix to form a soft dough. Knead the dough lightly on a floured surface to smooth.

Roll the dough out to an oblong about 12 by 9 inches. Trim the edges, reserving the trimmings. Brush the dough with the milk and sprinkle with the remaining Parmesan cheese. Cut the dough lengthwise into three equal strips, then cut across each strip to make ¼-inch-wide straws. Place the straws on the baking sheets, spaced slightly apart.

Bake in the oven until golden—10 to 15 minutes.

Carefully transfer the straws to wire racks to cool.

Meanwhile, reknead and reroll the reserved trimmings. Using a 2-inch plain round cutter, cut out rounds from the dough; then, using a 1¼-inch plain round cutter, cut out the center from each round to make a ring. Place the rings on a baking sheet. Reknead and reroll the trimmings. Cut out more rings in the same way, continuing until all of the dough is used up. Bake the rings until they are golden brown—six to eight minutes. Very carefully transfer the rings to wire racks to cool.

To serve, fill each ring with straws and arrange them on a serving platter; any remaining straws may be served separately.

Sesame Crackers

Makes about 100 crackers
Working time: about 30 minutes
Total time: about 55 minutes

Per 5 crackers:
Calories **95**
Protein **3g.**
Cholesterol **25mg.**
Total fat **5g.**
Saturated fat **3g.**
Sodium **70mg.**

2 cups unbleached all-purpose flour
¼ tsp. salt
¾ tsp. baking powder
4 tbsp. unsalted butter
3 oz. Cheddar cheese, finely grated (about ¾ cup)
1 small egg, beaten
2½ tbsp. sesame seeds

Preheat the oven to 400° F.
Grease several baking sheets.

Sift the flour, salt, and baking powder into a mixing bowl. Rub the butter into the flour until the mixture resembles fine breadcrumbs. Mix in the cheese, then make a well in the center of the flour. Pour 5 tablespoons of water into the well and mix with a wooden spoon to make a soft dough. Knead the dough on a lightly floured surface to smooth.

Roll the dough out very thin, then prick well all over with a fork. Using a 1¼-inch plain round cutter, cut out rounds from the dough and place them on baking sheets. Reknead and reroll the trimmings, then cut out more rounds. Continue until the dough is used up.

Brush the crackers with the beaten egg, then sprinkle with the sesame seeds. Bake in the oven until the crackers are golden brown and crisp—20 to 25 minutes. Place the crackers on wire racks to cool.

Chili and Lime Avocado Dip

Serves 12
Working time: about 15 minutes
Total time: about 3 hours and 15 minutes
(includes setting aside)

Calories **105**
Protein **2g.**
Cholesterol **0mg.**
Total fat **11g.**
Saturated fat **1g.**
Sodium **35mg.**

4 ripe avocados
1 tbsp. fresh lime juice
1 tbsp. virgin olive oil
1 pickled hot green chili pepper, finely diced (cautionary note, right)
1 garlic clove, crushed
1 scallion, finely chopped
1 tbsp. finely chopped cilantro
¼ tsp. salt
freshly ground black pepper

Cut the avocados in half and remove the pits. Spoon the flesh into a bowl and mash lightly with a fork—the texture should not be too smooth. Stir in the lime juice and oil, then the chili, garlic, scallion, cilantro, salt, and some freshly ground pepper.

Cover the mixture and set it aside for at least three hours to allow the chili to permeate the dip. Serve at room temperature.

SUGGESTED ACCOMPANIMENT: *breadsticks*.

Chili Peppers—a Cautionary Note

Both dried and fresh hot chili peppers should be handled with care. Their flesh and seeds contain volatile oils that can make skin tingle and cause eyes to burn. Rubber gloves offer protection—but the cook should still be careful not to touch the face, lips, or eyes when working with chilies.

Soaking fresh chilies in cold, salted water for an hour will remove some of their fire. If canned chilies are substituted for fresh ones, they should be rinsed in cold water in order to eliminate as much of the brine used to preserve them as possible.

Crudités on Skewers with Spiced Peanut Dip

Serves 10
Working time: about 2 hours
Total time: about 5 hours (includes chilling)

Calories **105**
Protein **5g.**
Cholesterol **2mg.**
Total fat **6g.**
Saturated fat **1g.**
Sodium **165mg.**

½ cup unsalted chicken stock (recipe, page 139)
1 tsp. saffron threads
¼ lb. (about 1 cup) peanuts
1 tbsp. virgin olive oil
1 large onion, very finely chopped
4 garlic cloves, crushed
1-inch piece fresh ginger, peeled and sliced
2 tsp. ground coriander
1 tsp. ground cumin
1 tsp. ground cardamom
1 cup plain low-fat yogurt
½ tsp. salt
freshly ground black pepper
2 tsp. finely cut fresh chives
1 tsp. finely chopped parsley

Crudités
1 medium daikon radish, peeled
12-16 radishes, trimmed
2 medium carrots, peeled
2 medium celery stalks, washed and trimmed
1 small sweet red pepper, seeded and deribbed
1 small green pepper, seeded and deribbed
1 small yellow pepper, seeded and deribbed
1 small orange pepper, seeded and deribbed (optional)

Preheat the oven to 425° F. In a saucepan, bring the chicken stock to a boil; remove the pan from the heat and add the saffron threads. Stir the stock well and let it stand for about 30 minutes.

Spread the peanuts out on a small baking sheet, then roast them in the oven for six to eight minutes.

Heat the oil in a saucepan; add the chopped onion, and cook over low heat until it is very soft but not browned—8 to 10 minutes. Stir in the garlic.

Put the ginger, coriander, cumin, cardamom, yogurt, peanuts, and saffron mixture into a blender or a food processor, and blend until smooth. Pour the mixture over the onions and stir well. Cook over low heat until the mixture thickens—about 20 minutes. Season with the salt and some pepper. Pour the mixture into a bowl and cover with plastic wrap, placing the wrap directly on the surface of the dip to prevent a skin from forming; allow to cool. Chill the dip in the refrigerator for three to four hours or overnight.

Just before serving time, prepare the vegetables. Cut them into decoratively shaped slices, as shown here, or small neat cubes, and thread them onto wooden cocktail sticks.

Stir the peanut dip and spoon it into a serving bowl, then sprinkle the top with the chives and parsley. Place the bowl on a large serving platter and surround with the crudités.

EDITOR'S NOTE: *If preferred, the vegetables may be cut into sticks, about 4 inches long, and arranged attractively around the peanut dip.*

Chickpea and Yogurt Dip

THIS RECIPE IS REMINISCENT OF THE MIDDLE EASTERN
DISH KNOWN AS HUMMUS.

Serves 6
Working time: about 15 minutes
Total time: about 2 hours (includes soaking)

Calories **145**
Protein **9g.**
Cholesterol **2mg.**
Total fat **3g.**
Saturated fat **trace**
Sodium **160mg.**

1 generous cup dried chickpeas
2 tbsp. tahini
½ cup plain low-fat yogurt
3 garlic cloves, crushed
2 lemons, juice only
½ tsp. salt
freshly ground black pepper
paprika for garnish
chopped parsley for garnish

Rinse the chickpeas under cold running water. Put them into a large, heavy-bottomed pan and pour in enough cold water to cover them by about 2 inches. Discard any chickpeas that float to the surface. Cover the pan, leaving the lid ajar, and bring the water to a boil; cook for two minutes. Turn off the heat, cover the pan, and soak the peas for at least one hour. (Alternatively, soak the chickpeas overnight in cold water.)

After soaking the chickpeas, drain them well in a colander. Return them to the pan and pour in enough water to cover them by about 2 inches. Bring the liquid to a simmer; cook the chickpeas over medium-low heat until they are quite tender—45 minutes to one hour. (If they appear to be drying out at any point, pour in more water.) When cooked, drain the peas and allow them to cool.

Place the chickpeas in a food processor with the tahini, yogurt, garlic, lemon juice, salt, and some pepper. Process for about 45 seconds to produce a soft, creamy paste. Transfer the dip to a shallow bowl, and sprinkle with some paprika and parsley before serving.

SUGGESTED ACCOMPANIMENT: *warmed pita bread, cut into fingers.*

Taramasalata

Serves 6
Working time: about 15 minutes
Total time: about 20 minutes

3 thick slices white bread (about 3 oz.), crusts removed
3 oz. codfish roe
2 oz. low-fat ricotta cheese
½ lemon, juice only
1 small garlic clove, crushed
freshly ground black pepper
lemon wedges for garnish

Calories **80**
Protein **6g.**
Cholesterol **0mg.**
Total fat **3g.**
Saturated fat **trace**
Sodium **120mg.**

Place the bread in a small bowl, cover with water, and let it soak for a few minutes.

Remove the bread from the water and squeeze it thoroughly dry, then place it in a food processor with the roe, ricotta cheese, lemon juice, garlic, and some black pepper. Process until smooth.

Transfer the purée to a small bowl and garnish with the lemon wedges.

SUGGESTED ACCOMPANIMENT: *warmed pita bread, cut into fingers.*

10 minutes. Immediately, pour off the boiling water and cool the eggs under cold running water.

Meanwhile, prepare the vegetables. Trim, wash, and dry the celery stalks. Cut the stalks into 6-inch evenly shaped lengths.

Cut one-half of the red pepper into matchstick-size strips; set aside 12 strips and chop the rest into small dice. Cut one-third of the green pepper into dice of the same size. (Reserve the remaining red and green pepper for another use.)

Shell the eggs, cut each one in half lengthwise, and remove the yolks. Sieve the egg yolks into a bowl, then sieve the ricotta cheese into the same bowl. Add the sour cream, salt, some pepper, and 2 tablespoons of the chives. Beat well together until the mixture is smooth and creamy.

Put the egg mixture into a pastry bag fitted with a medium-size star tip. Pipe a whirl of mixture into each egg white, then pipe the rest into the celery.

Sprinkle the eggs with the remaining chives and garnish each one with a twisted strip of red pepper. Sprinkle half of the celery with the chopped red pepper and the other half with the green pepper. Cut the celery into 1-inch lengths. Arrange the eggs and celery on serving platters.

Stuffed Eggs and Celery

Makes 60 pieces
Working (and total) time: about 40 minutes

Per piece:	
Calories **15**	6 eggs
Protein **1g.**	8 celery stalks
Cholesterol **10mg.**	1 small sweet red pepper, peeled (technique, right), seeded, and deribbed
Total fat **1g.**	
Saturated fat **trace**	1 small green pepper, peeled (technique, right), seeded, and deribbed
Sodium **30mg.**	
	⅓ cup low-fat ricotta cheese
	¼ cup sour cream
	¼ tsp. salt
	freshly ground black pepper
	3 tbsp. finely cut fresh chives

Put the eggs into a saucepan and cover them with cold water. Bring the water to a boil and cook the eggs for

Peeling Sweet Peppers

LOOSENING AND REMOVING THE SKIN. Place the pepper about 2 inches below a preheated broiler. Turn the pepper as its sides become slightly scorched; continue until the skin has blistered on all sides. Transfer the pepper to a bowl and cover with plastic wrap, or put the pepper into a paper bag and fold it shut; the trapped steam will make the pepper limp and loosen its skin. With a paring knife, peel off the pepper's skin in sections, from top to bottom. The pepper may then be seeded and deribbed.

Anise Crepe Fans with Herb Dip

Makes 24 crepe fans
Working time: about 30 minutes
Total time: about 1 hour

Per fan:
Calories **40**
Protein **1g.**
Cholesterol **10mg.**
Total fat **1g.**
Saturated fat **trace**
Sodium **5mg.**

1 cup unbleached all-purpose flour
¼ tsp. salt
1 egg
½ cup skim milk
1 tbsp. anise-flavored liqueur
1 tbsp. virgin olive oil
2 tbsp. chopped fresh chervil (optional)
¼ tsp. ground star anise (optional)
¼ tsp. safflower oil
Herb dip
½ cup plain low-fat yogurt
½ tbsp. mild grainy mustard
1 tsp. grated lemon zest
1 tsp. honey
2 tbsp. chopped fresh basil, or 6 leaves fresh, young sorrel, finely shredded

Sift the flour and salt into a mixing bowl. Make a well in the center of the flour, and add the egg and the skim milk. Pour in ½ cup of water, then beat the egg, milk, and water together with a wire whisk or a wooden spoon, gradually drawing in the flour. When no lumps remain, stir in the anise-flavored liqueur, olive oil, and the chervil and star anise, if you are using them. Let the mixture rest for about 30 minutes. The batter should be the consistency of thin cream; if it is thicker, add more water.

Heat a 10-inch crepe pan or nonstick frying pan *(box, page 86)* over medium-high heat. Add the safflower oil and spread it over the entire surface with a paper towel. Put about 3 tablespoons of the batter into the hot pan and immediately swirl the pan to coat the bottom with a thin, even layer of batter. Pour any excess batter back into the bowl. Cook the crepe until the bottom is browned—about 20 seconds. Lift the edge with a spatula and turn the crepe over. Cook the crepe on the second side until it, too, is browned—15 to 30 seconds. Slide the crepe onto a plate. Repeat the process with the remaining batter, stirring the batter between each crepe; if the pan looks dry, wipe it again with a little oil. Stack the cooked crepes on the plate as you go; cover them with a towel and set them aside. There should be enough batter to make six or seven anise crepes.

Preheat the oven to 375° F. Using a sharp knife or kitchen scissors, cut each crepe into quarters; fold each quarter in three, speckled side outward. Place the crepe fans on nonstick or lightly greased baking sheets, and bake until they are crisp on the outside— a little of the center will remain soft—about 15 minutes. Place the crepes on a wire rack to cool.

To make the herb dip, stir together the yogurt, mustard, lemon zest, honey, and basil or sorrel. Place the dip in a serving bowl and keep it in a cool place until serving time.

Labne Cocktail Balls

Makes about 24 labne balls
Working time: about 20 minutes
Total time: about 1 day (includes draining)

Per 3 balls:
Calories **70**
Protein **3g.**
Cholesterol **10mg.**
Total fat **3g.**
Saturated fat **2g.**
Sodium **35mg.**

1⅓ cups plain low-fat yogurt
2 tsp. coriander seeds, toasted and lightly crushed
2 tbsp. rolled oats, toasted
2 tsp. black poppy seeds, toasted
4 tbsp. finely chopped mixed fresh herbs such as parsley, chervil, mint, tarragon, and chives

To make the labne, line a large sieve with a double layer of cheesecloth or a large, round paper coffee filter. Place the sieve over a deep bowl and gently spoon the yogurt into the sieve. Cover the bowl and sieve with plastic wrap, and set aside for about two hours to start the initial separation of curds and whey. Then put the sieve and bowl into the refrigerator, and let the yogurt continue draining for about 24 hours to form a firm thick curd in the sieve.

When the labne is ready, add the crushed coriander seeds and mix well. Place the rolled oats on a shallow plate, the poppy seeds on another, and the fresh herbs on a third. Using a melon baller, a miniature ice-cream scoop, or two teaspoons, make small balls of curd and drop eight onto each of the coatings. Carefully roll the balls until they are well coated, then arrange them on a serving dish and refrigerate until needed.

EDITOR'S NOTE: *Labne may be made in advance and kept in the refrigerator, covered with plastic wrap, for two or three days. To toast coriander and poppy seeds, place them in a heavy-bottomed pan over high heat, and cook until they darken slightly, bounce, and release their aroma—one to two minutes; shake the pan to keep the seeds moving. Toast rolled oats in the same way until they are golden.*

Dates Stuffed with Bresaola and Mozzarella

Makes 30 stuffed dates
Working (and total) time: about 15 minutes

Per stuffed date:
Calories **20**
Protein **1g.**
Cholesterol **1mg.**
Total fat **2g.**
Saturated fat **1g.**
Sodium **40mg.**

1 tbsp. virgin olive oil
freshly ground black pepper
4½ oz. mozzarella, cut into 30 sticks about 2 by ½ by ½ inches
15 fresh dates, halved and pitted
1 oz. hard bresaola or prosciutto, cut into ½-inch-wide ribbons
fresh parsley sprigs for garnish

Pour the olive oil into a shallow dish, grind in some black pepper, and add the mozzarella sticks; carefully turn the cheese sticks in the oil to coat them thoroughly. Arrange the date halves, cut sides up, on a serving platter. Wind the ribbons of bresaola or prosciutto diagonally around the sticks of mozzarella, and lay them on the date halves. Serve the stuffed dates garnished with the sprigs of parsley.

Caviar Canapés

Makes 18 canapés
Working (and total) time: about 15 minutes

Per canapé:
Calories **20**
Protein **1g.**
Cholesterol **10mg.**
Total fat **1g.**
Saturated fat **trace**
Sodium **55mg.**

3 slices dark pumpernickel
½ cup sour cream
1 tbsp. black caviar or lumpfish roe
1 tbsp. red caviar or lumpfish roe

Cut each slice of dark pumpernickel in half lengthwise, then cut each half into thirds to make six 1½-inch squares. Arrange the pumpernickel squares on a serving dish or plate.

Spread a little of the sour cream onto the center of each piece of pumpernickel, leaving the edges of the bread showing. Spoon about ¼ teaspoon of black roe onto half the bread squares, then spoon a smaller amount of red roe onto the middle of the black roe. Spoon the red roe onto the remaining bread squares, with a smaller amount of black roe on top. Serve the canapés immediately.

Sesame Sushi

THE SUSHI IN THESE RECIPES IS WRAPPED IN NORI, A DARK GREEN SEAWEED SOLD PRESSED IN SHEETS AND DRIED, WHICH IS LIGHTLY TOASTED BEFORE USE.

Makes 16 sushi
Working time: about 40 minutes
Total time: about 1 hour and 30 minutes

Per sushi:
Calories **65**
Protein **2g.**
Cholesterol **0mg.**
Total fat **1g.**
Saturated fat **trace**
Sodium **75mg.**

1 cup sushi rice
1 tsp. salt
2 tsp. sugar
3 tbsp. rice vinegar
1 tbsp. sesame seeds
1 tsp. low-sodium soy sauce
⅛ tsp. wasabi powder
1 tbsp. dark tahini
2 sheets nori

Place the rice in a large bowl, add about five times its volume of cold water, stir gently, then carefully pour off the water. Repeat the rinsing twice more to wash away excess starch. Drain the rice and leave it in a sieve for about 45 minutes to allow the grains to absorb any residual water.

Put the rice into a saucepan with 1 cup of water and bring to a boil, partially covered, over high heat. Reduce the heat to very low, cover, and simmer for 10 minutes. Leave the pan on the stove, with the heat turned off, for another 10 to 15 minutes. Dissolve the salt and sugar in 2 tablespoons of the vinegar, and mix into the cooked rice with a wet wooden spoon.

Place the sesame seeds in a heavy-bottomed frying pan, and toast over medium heat, stirring the seeds, until they are golden—two to three minutes.

Mix 2 teaspoons of the vinegar, the soy sauce, wasabi powder, and tahini into a paste; add a little more vinegar if necessary to give a creamy consistency. In a small bowl, mix the remaining vinegar with 3 tablespoons of water. Toast one sheet of nori by waving it about 5 inches above a high flame for a few seconds, until it turns papery, then lay it out on a bamboo rolling mat with a longer edge toward you. Moisten your fingers in the bowl of water and vinegar, and use them to spread half of the rice over the nori. (Moisture from the rice will soften the nori.) Spread the rice evenly up to the two long sides of the nori, and firm it down with your fingertips.

Using a palette knife or the back of a spoon, spread half of the tahini paste over the rice. Reserve some of the sesame seeds for a garnish, then sprinkle half of the remaining seeds evenly on top of the paste.

With the help of the rolling mat, roll up the covered sheet of nori *(technique, page 28)*. Toast the second sheet of nori, spread it with the remaining rice, tahini paste, and sesame seeds, and roll it up in the same way. Cut each roll into eight pieces, wiping the knife with a damp cloth after each cut. Place the slices on a serving plate and sprinkle the reserved sesame seeds over them, following the spiral pattern.

EDITOR'S NOTE: *Italian short-grain rice may be used instead of sushi rice. Dry mustard may be substituted for wasabi powder. Sheets of nori for making sushi—labeled yaki sushi nori—come in a standard size of 8 by 7 inches. Bamboo rolling mats are sold in Japanese groceries; a small rush table mat, or several layers of parchment paper, may be used instead.*

Avocado Sushi with Olives and Peppers

Makes 24 sushi
Working time: about 50 minutes
Total time: about 1 hour and 20 minutes

Per sushi:
Calories **40**
Protein **1g.**
Cholesterol **0mg.**
Total fat **2g.**
Saturated fat **trace**
Sodium **35mg.**

¾ cup sushi rice
½ tsp. salt
1½ tsp. sugar
1 lemon, juice strained, zest of one-quarter removed with a peeler
2 scallions
½ small firm avocado
½ small sweet red pepper, peeled (technique, page 22), seeded, and deribbed
20 black olives, pitted
⅛ tsp. wasabi powder
1 tsp. rice vinegar
4 sheets nori

Put the rice into a large bowl and add about fives times its volume of water. Stir gently, then carefully pour off the water. Repeat the rinsing twice, then drain the rice and leave it in a sieve for about 45 minutes to allow the grains to absorb any residual water.

Put the rice into a saucepan with 1 cup of water and bring to a boil, partially covered, over high heat. Reduce the heat to very low, cover the pan, and simmer for 10 minutes. Leave the pan on the stove, with the heat turned off, for 10 to 15 minutes. Dissolve the salt and sugar in 2 tablespoons of the lemon juice, and mix into the rice with a wet wooden spoon.

Blanch the lemon zest in boiling water for five seconds, refresh in cold water, then drain and dry the zest with paper towels. Cut the lemon zest and the scallions into fine slivers. Peel the avocado and cut the flesh into ¼-inch-wide strips. Toss the avocado strips gently with 1 teaspoon of the remaining lemon juice to prevent them from discoloring. Cut the pepper into narrow strips. Cut the olives in half lengthwise. Mix the wasabi powder with a little water to make a paste.

In a small bowl, mix the vinegar with 3 tablespoons of water. Trim off one-third of each nori sheet with kitchen scissors along a long edge, and discard. Divide the rice into four portions. Toast one piece of nori by waving it about 5 inches above a high flame for a few seconds, until it turns papery, then lay it out on a bamboo rolling mat with a long edge toward you. Moisten your fingers in the bowl of vinegar and water. Starting at the edge nearest you, spread one portion of the rice over about three-quarters of a toasted nori sheet, firming the rice with your fingertips. (Moisture from the rice will soften the nori.)

Spread a layer of wasabi paste along the middle of the rice. Place one-quarter of the olive halves end to end on the wasabi paste, one-quarter of the avocado strips on top of the olives, then add one-quarter of the pepper strips, slivers of scallion, and lemon zest. With the help of the rolling mat, roll up the covered sheet of nori *(technique, page 28);* the uncovered strip will wrap around the roll, adhering to itself.

Repeat with the remaining nori and filling ingredients to make three more rolls. Cut each roll into six slices, wiping the knife with a damp cloth after each cut, and arrange the slices on a serving plate.

EDITOR'S NOTE: *Italian short-grain rice may replace sushi rice. Dry mustard may be substituted for wasabi powder.*

Rolling Sushi

1 STARTING THE ROLLING. Place a slatted mat on the work surface; lay a sheet of nori seaweed at one end of the mat, parallel with the slats. Following the recipe, arrange the sushi ingredients on the nori sheet. Carefully lift up the end of the mat and turn the end over the ingredients to begin the roll.

2 COMPLETING THE ROLL. Roll the mat away from you, pressing with your fingers and palms to make a cylinder. Use the mat to roll the cylinder backward and forward several times to compact the rice.

Prunes Stuffed with Wild Rice and Turkey

Makes 14 stuffed prunes
Working time: about 30 minutes
Total time: about 1 hour and 30 minutes

Per stuffed prune:
Calories **25**
Protein **2g.**
Cholesterol **5mg.**
Total fat **trace**
Saturated fat **trace**
Sodium **30mg.**

2 tbsp. wild rice
1 cup unsalted chicken stock (recipe, page 139) or water
14 large ready-to-eat prunes
2 oz. smoked turkey or chicken, finely chopped
freshly grated nutmeg
¼ tsp. salt
freshly ground black pepper
1 tbsp. finely cut chives

Put the rice and stock or water into a heavy-bottomed saucepan, bring to a boil, then simmer, covered, until the husks of the rice have split—50 to 60 minutes. Drain off any remaining cooking liquid and set the rice aside to cool.

Using a sharp knife, slit open one side of each prune from end to end. Mix the turkey or chicken with the rice, season with some nutmeg, the salt, and some pepper, and stuff the prunes with this mixture. Sprinkle the chives over the stuffed prunes and serve.

EDITOR'S NOTE: *The prunes in this recipe are sold for eating straight from the packet and do not require presoaking or pitting. If you use ordinary prunes, soak them in boiling water and a dash of Madeira for 10 minutes, and then pit them.*

Puffs with Mushroom and Pine-Nut Filling

Makes 30 puffs
Working time: about 1 hour and 10 minutes
Total time: about 1 hour and 30 minutes

Per puff:	
Calories **50**	4 tbsp. unsalted butter
Protein **2g.**	⅔ cup unbleached all-purpose flour
Cholesterol **25mg.**	¼ tsp. salt
Total fat **4g.**	2 eggs
Saturated fat **2g.**	paprika for garnish
Sodium **40mg.**	**Mushroom filling**
	2 tbsp. unsalted butter
	1½ lb. mushrooms, coarsely chopped
	1 small onion or 4 shallots, chopped
	1 garlic clove, crushed
	2 tbsp. finely chopped fresh tarragon, or 1 tbsp. finely chopped fresh dill
	½ tsp. grated nutmeg
	¼ tsp. salt
	freshly ground black pepper
	1 tbsp. dry sherry or brandy
	1 tbsp. sherry vinegar
	2 tbsp. fine fresh breadcrumbs
	¼ cup pine nuts, lightly toasted

First, make the filling. Melt the butter in a heavy frying pan over medium heat; add the mushrooms and sauté them for two to three minutes. Add the onion or shallots, garlic, tarragon or dill, nutmeg, salt, and some pepper, and continue to sauté until the mushrooms are soft—7 to 10 minutes.

Using a slotted spoon, transfer the mushrooms to a food processor, leaving the cooking juices in the pan. Add the sherry or brandy and the sherry vinegar to the juices, and reduce rapidly over high heat until only about 2 tablespoons remain.

Add the liquid to the mushrooms. Process until smooth, then add the breadcrumbs and pine nuts, and process again. Check the consistency of the mixture: It should be quite dry; otherwise, the puffs will become soggy when they are filled. If necessary, add more breadcrumbs. Chill the filling in the refrigerator while you make the puffs.

Preheat the oven to 425° F. Line a large baking sheet with foil or parchment paper.

To make the dough, put the butter and ½ cup of water into a saucepan, and set over low heat to melt the butter without evaporating any water. Then bring the butter and water to a boil, remove from the heat, and add the flour and salt, stirring continuously with a wooden spoon. Return the pan to low heat and cook until the mixture forms a ball in the center of the pan. Remove the pan from the heat, let the dough cool for a few minutes, then add the eggs one at a time, mixing well after each addition.

Using a pastry bag fitted with a ½-inch plain tip, make 30 little mounds that are about ¾ inch in diameter on the prepared baking sheet, spaced apart. Alternatively, use a teaspoon to make the shapes. Lightly flatten any little ripples or peaks with a wet teaspoon or finger.

Bake the puffs until they are well risen and golden brown on the sides as well as on top—20 to 25 minutes. Remove the puffs from the oven and pierce each with a small pointed knife to allow the steam to escape, then return them to the oven for four to five minutes to dry out completely. Transfer the puffs to a wire rack to cool.

Fill the puffs as near to serving time as possible. Slice off the top third of each puff and place a teaspoon of the mushroom filling inside. Replace the tops. Using a fine-mesh sieve or a tea strainer, sprinkle a little paprika on top of each puff.

EDITOR'S NOTE: *If you wish to serve the puffs warm, fill them as described above, then heat them in a 425° F. oven for five to six minutes.*

Crepe Cups with Green Pea and Mushroom Filling

Makes about 36 cups
Working time: about 40 minutes
Total time: about 1 hour and 20 minutes

Per cup:
Calories **30**
Protein **1g.**
Cholesterol **5mg.**
Total fat **1g.**
Saturated fat **0g.**
Sodium **30mg.**

1 cup unbleached all-purpose flour
¼ tsp. salt
1 egg
¾ cup skim milk
½ cup light beer
1 tbsp. light sesame oil
½ tsp. safflower oil
Green pea and mushroom filling
½ lb. fresh green peas, or ½ lb. frozen green peas, thawed
½ oz. fresh chervil or parsley
½ cup plain low-fat yogurt
1 tbsp. grainy mustard
¼ tsp. salt
8 oz. tiny mushrooms, wiped clean and quartered

To make the crepe batter, sift the flour and salt into a bowl. Make a well in the center of the flour, and add the egg, milk, and most of the beer. Beat the liquid ingredients together with a wire whisk or a wooden spoon, gradually drawing in the flour, until no lumps remain. Stir in the sesame oil and let the batter rest for about 30 minutes. It should be the consistency of thin cream; if it is too thick, add the remaining beer.

Preheat the oven to 375° F.

Heat a large crepe or nonstick frying pan over medium-high heat. Pour in the safflower oil and spread it over the entire surface with a paper towel. Drop 1 tablespoon of the batter onto the pan, and use the back of a spoon to spread the batter into a round of about 3 inches in diameter. Form two or three more crepes until the pan is filled. Cook until the bottoms are browned—about one minute—then turn the crepes with a spatula and cook them until the second sides are browned—15 to 30 seconds. Slide the crepes onto a plate. Repeat with the remaining batter, brushing the pan lightly with a little more oil if the crepes begin to stick. Stack the cooked crepes on the plate as you go. Cover the crepes with a dishtowel and set them aside. There should be about 36.

Place the crepes inside 3½-inch-diameter brioche pans or muffin cups. (The pans do not require greasing, even if they are not nonstick.) Bake the pancakes until they are crisp—10 to 15 minutes; check them as they cook to ensure that the edges do not burn. Then place the pancake cups on a wire rack to cool.

While the crepe cups are baking, prepare the filling. Bring 1 quart of water to a boil in a saucepan. Cook the fresh peas in the water until barely tender—three to four minutes—then drain them. (If you are using frozen peas, cook them in ¼ cup of boiling water for 10 seconds.) Set aside some chervil or parsley leaves for garnish, then finely chop the remaining leaves and blend with the yogurt, mustard, and salt. Stir the peas into the yogurt mixture together with the mushrooms.

Fill the pancake cups with the pea and mushroom filling just before serving; the cups will become soft if they are filled in advance. Garnish with the reserved chervil or parsley leaves.

Stuffed Cherry Tomatoes

Makes 20 stuffed tomatoes
Working (and total) time: about 30 minutes

Per stuffed tomato:	*20 cherry tomatoes*
Calories **20**	*⅓ cup low-fat ricotta cheese*
Protein **1g.**	*2 tsp. chopped fresh basil*
Cholesterol **trace**	*⅛ tsp. salt*
Total fat **2g.**	*freshly ground black pepper*
Saturated fat **0g.**	*parsley leaves for garnish*
Sodium **25mg.**	

Slice the bottoms off the cherry tomatoes, and using
a small melon baller or a teaspoon, scoop out the seeds
and juice into a sieve placed over a small bowl. Press
the juice from the seeds and discard the seeds. Mix the
cheese with the basil, salt, some freshly ground pepper, and about 3 teaspoons of the tomato juice to
make a soft paste.

Using a pastry bag fitted with a ½-inch star tip, pipe
a rosette of the cheese mixture into each tomato.
Garnish each filled tomato with a tiny piece of parsley
and arrange the tomatoes on a serving plate.

Snow Peas with Two Purées

Makes about 36 snow peas
Working time: about 30 minutes
Total time: about 45 minutes

Per 3 carrot snow peas: Calories **25** Protein **2g.** Cholesterol **0mg.** Total fat **trace** Saturated fat **trace** Sodium **20mg.**	*4 oz. snow peas*
	Cumin-scented carrot purée
	2 small carrots, peeled and sliced into ¼-inch rounds
	¼ tsp. ground cumin
	1 tbsp. sour cream
	2 tsp. fresh breadcrumbs
	⅛ tsp. salt
	ground white pepper
Per 3 pea snow peas: Calories **40** Protein **3g.** Cholesterol **2mg.** Total fat **1g.** Saturated fat **trace** Sodium **15mg.**	**Minted pea purée**
	3 shallots, finely chopped
	1 tsp. unsalted butter
	12 oz. fresh peas, shelled, or 4 oz. frozen peas, thawed
	½ tsp. finely chopped fresh mint
	1 tbsp. sour cream
	2 tsp. fresh breadcrumbs
	⅛ tsp. salt

Place the snow peas in a deep, ovenproof bowl and pour boiling water over them. Drain immediately in a colander and refresh them under cold running water.

Leave the snow peas in the colander to drain.

To make the carrot purée, put the carrots into a saucepan with enough cold water to barely cover them; add the cumin, bring to a boil, and cook until the carrots are soft—7 to 10 minutes. Drain over a bowl. Return the cooking liquid to the pan and reduce over high heat until only about a teaspoonful remains. Purée the carrots with the reduced cooking liquid in a blender, food processor, or food mill. Pass the purée through a fine sieve if a smoother texture is preferred. If the purée is watery, cook it briefly in a saucepan over very low heat to dry it out a little. Stir in the sour cream and breadcrumbs, season with the salt and some white pepper, then set the mixture aside.

For the pea purée, sweat the shallots in the butter until they are translucent. Add the peas and 2 table-spoons of water. Heat over low heat until the water has completely evaporated, then remove from the heat, add the mint, and stir well. Purée the peas in a food processor or a blender, and stir in the sour cream, breadcrumbs, and salt. Set the mixture aside.

Arrange the snow peas on serving dishes. Using a pastry bag fitted with a fine tip, pipe the carrot purée in a line down the center of half of the snow peas. Then pipe the pea purée onto the remaining snow peas. Serve the snow peas cold.

Artichoke-Stuffed Mushrooms

Makes 20 mushrooms
Working time: about 30 minutes
Total time: about 40 minutes

Per mushroom:
Calories **20**
Protein **trace**
Cholesterol **0mg.**
Total fat **2g.**
Saturated fat **1g.**
Sodium **35mg.**

20 large, white mushrooms, wiped clean, stems removed
1 lemon, juice only
2 tbsp. polyunsaturated margarine
Artichoke stuffing
4 small or 2 large artichokes trimmed down to the hearts, chokes removed
2 tsp. red wine vinegar
½ tsp. Dijon mustard
¼ tsp. salt
freshly ground black pepper
1 garlic clove, crushed
¼ tsp. ground cardamom
1 tbsp. virgin olive oil
1 tbsp. chopped flat-leaf parsley, plus flat-leaf parsley sprigs for garnish

Put the mushrooms into a large bowl with the lemon juice. Toss the mixture gently together and set aside for 5 to 10 minutes.

Cook the artichoke hearts in boiling water until they are tender—five to six minutes. Drain in a colander and refresh them under cold running water. Drain well and set the artichoke hearts aside.

Melt the margarine in a wide sauté pan or frying pan with a lid. Place the mushrooms in a single layer in the pan, rounded sides down. Cover and cook until they just begin to soften—two to three minutes. (Do not overcook, because they will loose their shape.) Using a slotted spoon, lift the mushrooms from the pan onto paper towels to drain and cool.

Put the vinegar, mustard, salt, some pepper, garlic, cardamom, oil, and parsley into a bowl, and whisk together. Finely chop the artichoke hearts and add them to the bowl. Mix well.

Spoon the artichoke mixture into the mushrooms, forming neat mounds. Garnish each one with a tiny sprig of parsley, then arrange the mushrooms neatly on a serving dish.

EDITOR'S NOTE: *The mushroom caps may be left uncooked.*

Citrus Seviche Skewers

SEVICHE IS A SPANISH WORD FOR MARINATED RAW FISH.

Makes 60 sticks
Working time: about 1 hour
Total time: about 6 hours (includes marinating)

Per 3 sticks:
Calories **25**
Protein **5g.**
Cholesterol **15mg.**
Total fat **1g.**
Saturated fat **trace**
Sodium **70mg.**

1 lb. haddock fillets
½ cucumber
¼ tsp. salt
3 large oranges
1 tbsp. virgin olive oil
1 tsp. Dijon mustard
freshly ground black pepper
2 tbsp. chopped fresh basil, or 2 tsp. dried basil
Citrus marinade
1 tbsp. virgin olive oil
2 tbsp. fresh lemon juice, strained
2 tbsp. fresh lime juice, strained
2 tbsp. chopped parsley
¼ tsp. salt
freshly ground black pepper

Rinse the fillets under cold running water and pat them dry with paper towels. Using a very sharp knife, carefully remove the skin from the fillets and remove any visible bones. Cut the fillets lengthwise into strips about ½ inch wide, then cut across the strips to make 60 squares. Remove any remaining bones.

To make the marinade, put the oil, lemon and lime juice, parsley, salt, and some pepper into a shallow,

nonreactive dish, and whisk together. Add the haddock pieces and turn to coat them well. Cover the dish and put it in the refrigerator. Marinate the fish for at least five hours, turning the pieces two or three times.

About one hour before you are ready to assemble the seviche skewers, prepare the cucumber and oranges. Remove the skin from the cucumber, then cut it in half lengthwise and scoop out the seeds. Cut each piece of cucumber in half again lengthwise, then cut into ¼-inch-thick slices. Put the cucumber into a bowl and sprinkle with the salt. Cover and set aside for about 30 minutes.

Using a small knife, remove the skin and all of the white pith from the oranges. Holding each orange over a small bowl to catch the juice, slice between flesh and membrane to remove the segments. Cut each segment into two or three pieces, depending on the size of the orange, to make 60 pieces in all. Put the oil, mustard, some pepper, and 1 tablespoon of the orange juice into a bowl. Whisk together, then stir in the basil. Add the orange segments and mix gently until they are well coated. Cover and set aside until needed.

To assemble the seviche skewers, thoroughly drain the marinated haddock and the salted cucumber. Thread the haddock, cucumber, and orange segments onto cocktail sticks. Arrange neatly in a shallow bowl, or spear into large oranges. Keep the seviche skewers refrigerated until ready to serve.

Codfish-Roe Canapés

Makes 24 canapés
Working (and total) time: about 25 minutes

Per canapé:
Calories **20**
Protein **1g.**
Cholesterol **30mg.**
Total fat **1g.**
Saturated fat **0g.**
Sodium **35mg.**

½ lb. codfish roe
½ tsp. Dijon mustard
1 tbsp. sour cream
½ tsp. fresh lemon juice
2 tsp. finely cut chives, plus a few chives for garnish
⅛ tsp. cayenne pepper
1 small loaf dark rye bread, cut into thin slices
24 small capers, rinsed and drained

Mix the codfish roe with the mustard, sour cream, lemon juice, cut chives, and cayenne pepper. Using a 1½-inch round fluted pastry cutter, cut out 24 rounds from the rye bread.

Spread the codfish-roe mixture on the circles of bread, and garnish each canapé with a caper and a few of the chives.

Arrange the canapés decoratively on a serving plate.

Anchovy Toasts

Makes 16 toasts
Working time: about 15 minutes
Total time: about 40 minutes

Per toast:
Calories **50**
Protein **1g.**
Cholesterol **5mg.**
Total fat **4g.**
Saturated fat **1g.**
Sodium **180mg.**

4 thin slices bread
1½ oz. small anchovy fillets, rinsed and drained
2 tbsp. polyunsaturated margarine
½ tsp. fresh lemon juice
⅛ tsp. cayenne pepper
freshly ground black pepper
parsley or lemon wedges for garnish (optional)

Preheat the oven to 350° F.

Cut out a diamond-shaped piece of cardboard with 2-inch-long sides, and use this template to cut 16 diamonds from the slices of bread. Place the bread diamonds on a baking sheet in the oven until they are golden on both sides, turning if necessary—about 25 minutes. Set aside to cool.

Reserve four whole anchovy fillets and pound the rest in a mortar until a smooth paste is obtained. Gradually beat in the margarine, and season with the lemon juice, cayenne pepper, and some black pepper.

Spread the anchovy mixture evenly onto the diamond toasts, then draw the tines of a fork through the mixture to produce decorative lines. Cut each of the reserved anchovies into four long, thin strips. Twist each strip and lay it on top of a toast. Serve garnished with parsley or lemon wedges, if you like.

Green-Jacket Rock Shrimp

Makes 12 rock shrimp
Working time: about 35 minutes
Total time: about 45 minutes

Per shrimp:
Calories **30**
Protein **4g.**
Cholesterol **25g.**
Total fat **0g.**
Saturated fat **0g.**
Sodium **200mg.**

12 live or frozen rock shrimp or large shrimp (about 1½ lb.)
12 spinach leaves, about 4 inches long
3 tbsp. low-sodium soy sauce
3 tbsp. mirin
3 tsp. wasabi powder (optional)
Poaching liquid
½ cup dry white wine
1 small onion or shallot, sliced
1 carrot, diced
2 celery stalks, diced
1 bay leaf
5 sprigs parsley
2 sprigs fresh thyme or dill
1 tsp. salt
5 black peppercorns

To make the poaching liquid, pour 2 quarts of water into a large, nonreactive saucepan, and add the wine, onion or shallot, carrot, celery, bay leaf, parsley, thyme or dill, salt, and peppercorns. Bring the liquid to a boil,

lower the heat, and simmer for 10 minutes. Rinse the shrimp under cold running water, then put them into the liquid; cover and simmer for three to four minutes.

While the shrimp are cooking, prepare the spinach leaves. Wash the leaves thoroughly, blanch for 30 seconds in boiling water, then refresh in cold water and drain well. Remove the central rib from each leaf, and fold the leaf lengthwise to form a ribbon about half as wide as the length of a shrimp.

As soon as the shrimp are cooked, rinse them under cold running water. Twist off the heads, legs, and front claws, and discard. Using a sharp pair of scissors, slit the underside of the shell along the belly of the shellfish up to the tail fins. Using a sharp knife, remove the dark vein. Remove most of the shell, leaving only the tail fins intact. If using large shrimp, peel them, leaving the tail intact, and devein if necessary.

Combine the soy sauce and mirin in a small bowl, and dip each shrimp in the mixture. Wrap the end opposite the tail in a spinach-leaf ribbon, leaving the tail fins and a little of the body exposed. (The spinach will adhere to itself.) Arrange the shrimp on a serving dish. Serve the remaining soy sauce and mirin mixture as a dip, and for those who like spicy food, serve the wasabi powder in a separate bowl.

Smoked Salmon Roll-Ups

Makes 16 roll-ups
Working (and total) time: about 30 minutes

Per roll-up:
Calories **30**
Protein **3g.**
Cholesterol **5mg.**
Total fat **1g.**
Saturated fat **trace**
Sodium **180mg.**

1 tbsp. dill, finely chopped
freshly ground black pepper
3 tbsp. sour cream
4 oz. smoked salmon, cut into 16 thin strips about 3 by 2 inches each
16 canned or frozen baby corn
16 chives or slivers of scallion
lime wedges for garnish

To make the sour-cream spread, blend the dill and a few generous grindings of black pepper into the sour cream, and coat one side of each strip of smoked salmon with a little of this mixture.

Roll a strip of smoked salmon around each ear of baby corn, and tie a chive or sliver of scallion around the salmon. Serve garnished with the lime wedges.

EDITOR'S NOTE: *Canned baby corn requires no cooking; for frozen baby corn, cook according to the directions on the back of the package.*

Sushi of Shrimp and Seaweed in Radicchio

THIS RECIPE CALLS FOR WAKAME, A GREEN SEAWEED COMMON IN JAPAN. SOLD DRIED IN HEALTH-FOOD STORES AND JAPANESE GROCERIES, IT MUST BE SOAKED BRIEFLY BEFORE USE.

Makes 24 sushi
Working time: about 30 minutes
Total time: about 1 hour and 20 minutes

Per sushi:
Calories **40**
Protein **1g.**
Cholesterol **5mg.**
Total fat **trace**
Saturated fat **trace**
Sodium **75mg.**

1 cup sushi rice
1 tsp. salt
2 tsp. sugar
2 tbsp. plus 1 tsp. rice vinegar
24 chives, or 2 scallions cut into very fine ribbons
3 oz. large shrimp, peeled, deveined if necessary, and cooked
⅛ tsp. wasabi powder
1½ tsp. dried wakame
12 large radicchio leaves

Put the rice into a large bowl and add about five times its volume of water. Stir gently, then carefully pour off the water. Repeat the rinsing twice, then drain the rice and leave it in a sieve for about 45 minutes to allow the grains to absorb any residual water.

Put the rice into a saucepan with 1 cup of water and bring to a boil, partially covered, over high heat. Reduce the heat to very low, cover the pan, and simmer for 10 minutes. Leave the pan on the stove, with the heat turned off, for 10 to 15 minutes. Dissolve the salt and sugar in 2 tablespoons of the vinegar, and mix into the rice with a wet wooden spoon.

While the rice is being prepared, blanch the chives or scallions by pouring boiling water over them in a bowl. Refresh immediately in cold water, drain, then dry on paper towels. Dice the shrimp. Mix the wasabi powder with a little water to make a paste. Soak the wakame in water for 5 to 10 minutes—it will quadruple in size—then squeeze it dry in a dishtowel.

Halve each radicchio leaf lengthwise and trim away the thick, white center ribs. Mix the remaining vinegar with 3 tablespoons of water in a bowl; dip your fingers in the bowl and spread the rice over three-quarters of the length of each leaf with your fingers, pressing it down. Spread a thin layer of wasabi paste over the rice, followed by the wakame, and then the shrimp.

Roll up each leaf to enclose the rice and filling, wrapping the empty quarter of the leaf neatly around the roll. Tie a ribbon of chive or scallion around each sushi to secure it, and trim the sides with a sharp knife. Arrange the sushi on serving plates.

EDITOR'S NOTE: *Italian short-grain rice may replace sushi rice. Dry mustard may be substituted for wasabi powder.*

Lemon and Tarragon Scallop Croustades

Makes 24 croustades
Working time: about 20 minutes
Total time: about 30 minutes

Per croustade:
Calories **20**
Protein **1g.**
Cholesterol **5mg.**
Total fat **1g.**
Saturated fat **0g.**
Sodium **45mg.**

6 slices whole-wheat bread
1 tbsp. polyunsaturated margarine, melted
Scallop filling
4 tsp. arrowroot
⅓ cup clam juice
6 sea scallops, bright white connective tissue removed
½ tsp. grated lemon zest, plus ½ tsp. fresh lemon juice
1 tsp. finely chopped fresh tarragon
freshly ground black pepper
1 tsp. light cream or milk
fresh tarragon sprigs for garnish
thin strips of lemon zest for garnish

Preheat the oven to 425° F. Flatten the bread slices with a rolling pin. Using a 2½-inch daisy cutter, cut out 24 shapes. Brush 24 small muffin cups, about 1½ inches in diameter, with some of the margarine, and press the bread into the cups. Brush the cases with the remaining margarine and bake them until they are crisp—about 10 minutes. Set aside to cool.

To prepare the filling, place the arrowroot in a small bowl and blend it with 2 tablespoons of the clam juice.

Pour the remaining clam juice into a small saucepan and bring to a boil; add the scallops and simmer, covered, for two minutes. Remove the scallops with a slotted spoon, dice them, and set aside.

Pour the arrowroot mixture into the warm clam juice and stir. Add the grated lemon zest and juice, tarragon, and some pepper. Bring to a boil and cook for one minute, then remove the pan from the heat, and stir in the cream or milk and scallops. Arrange the bread cases on a serving plate. Divide the filling among them, and garnish with the tarragon sprigs and strips of lemon zest. Serve at room temperature.

Stuffed Squid Rings

Makes 32 rings
Working time: about 30 minutes
Total time: about 1 hour 15 minutes

Per ring:
Calories **15**
Protein **3g.**
Cholesterol **35g.**
Total fat **trace**
Saturated fat **trace**
Sodium **25mg.**

8 small young squid (about 1 lb.), cleaned and skinned (technique, opposite)	
8 leaves bib or other crisp lettuce, washed and dried	
3½ oz. turbot or halibut fillet, skinned and diced	

1 cup unsalted fish or vegetable stock (recipes, page 139)
2 tbsp. low-sodium soy sauce
1-inch piece fresh ginger, finely sliced
1 tbsp. molasses
1 tbsp. balsamic vinegar, or ½ tbsp. red wine vinegar

Drain and dry the squid tentacles and pouches with paper towels. Spread open a lettuce leaf and trim it to the same length as one of the pouches. Place a set of tentacles along the center line of the leaf, and arrange one-eighth of the diced fillet on the leaf at the tentacle tips. Roll up the leaf tightly and place the lettuce package inside one of the pouches. Trim away any excess leaf and secure the pouch opening with a cocktail stick. Stuff the remaining pouches in the same way.

Combine the stock, low-sodium soy sauce, ginger, molasses, and vinegar in a saucepan or a flameproof casserole, and bring to a boil. Add the stuffed squid, cover, and simmer gently until the squid are tender—30 to 45 minutes. Since both squid and lettuce will shrink considerably, releasing juices as they cook, turning should not be necessary; but check occasionally that all surfaces are covered by liquid, and add more water if they are not. Allow the squid to cool in their liquid, then chill them in the refrigerator.

Shortly before serving time, drain the squid and remove the cocktail sticks. Slice each pouch into four thick rings.

SUGGESTED ACCOMPANIMENT: *small crisp lettuce leaves, for easy handling.*

Preparing Squid for Cooking

1 *SEPARATING THE POUCH AND TENTACLES. Working over a bowl of water or a sink, hold the squid's pouch in one hand and its tentacles in the other. Gently pull the tentacles until the viscera separate from the inside of the pouch. Place the tentacles, with the head and viscera still attached, in the bowl.*

2 *REMOVING THE PEN. Feel inside the pouch with your fingers to locate the pen, or quill—a cartilaginous structure running nearly the length of the pouch. Pull out the pen and discard it. Reach inside the pouch and scrape out any remaining gelatinous material with your fingers; wash the pouch thoroughly.*

3 *SKINNING THE POUCH. Carefully pull off the edible triangular fins on either side of the pouch and skin them. Starting at the open end of the pouch, use your fingers to pull the mottled purplish skin away from the pale flesh. Continue peeling off the skin from the pouch; discard the skin. Rinse the pouch and fins, then set them aside in a bowl of fresh cold water.*

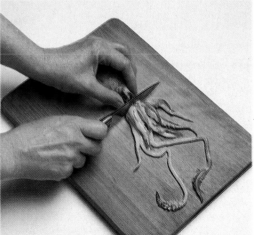

4 *CUTTING OFF THE TENTACLES. Lay the viscera, head, and tentacles on a cutting board. Sever the tentacles from the head below the eyes; the tentacles should remain joined together by a narrow band of flesh. Discard the head and viscera. If any of the bony beak remains in the tentacle section, squeeze it out.*

Roulade of Salmon and Sole Filled with Spinach

Makes about 35 slices
Working time: about 45 minutes
Total time: about 4 hours (includes chilling)

Per slice:
Calories **30**
Protein **4g.**
Cholesterol **15mg.**
Total fat **2g.**
Saturated fat **trace**
Sodium **70mg.**

12 oz. salmon fillets
10 oz. Dover sole or halibut fillets, skinned
12 oz. spinach, washed and stemmed
1 lemon, coarsely sliced
1 onion, coarsely chopped
2 carrots, coarsely sliced
2 tsp. black peppercorns
1 oz. parsley sprigs
2 cups white wine vinegar
1 tsp. chopped fresh dill
1 tsp. salt
2½ qt. unsalted fish stock (recipe, page 139) or water

Remove all the bones from the salmon and trim any membrane. Using a sharp, thin-bladed knife, cut thin horizontal slices from the fillets, working toward the skin. In the center of a piece of wet cheesecloth about 20 by 12 inches, lay the slices of salmon to form a rectangle measuring 14 by 8 inches; fill any gaps with odd bits of salmon. Slice the sole or halibut fillets in the same way, and lay the slices on top of the salmon to cover it completely.

Plunge the spinach into a saucepan of boiling water and cook for 20 seconds. Drain the spinach, squeeze out as much water as possible, and chop it coarsely. Arrange the spinach along one long edge of the fish rectangle in the shape of a cylinder that is about ¾ inch in diameter.

With both hands, grip the edge of the cheesecloth nearest the spinach. Pull the cheesecloth toward you and gently lift it, a little at a time, gradually rolling the fish around the spinach. Continue lifting and rolling until the roll is complete. Wrap the cheesecloth around the completed roll and secure it at each end with string. Tie 1-inch-wide strips of cheesecloth around the roll at intervals of about 2 inches.

To prepare a court-bouillon, place the lemon, onion, carrots, peppercorns, parsley, vinegar, dill, and salt in a fish poacher or roasting pan long enough to accommodate the salmon roll. Add fish stock to a depth of about 3 inches so that the roll will be completely covered when it is put into the pan. Bring the stock to a boil, then lower the heat until it is just simmering. Carefully place the cheesecloth-wrapped roll in the court-bouillon and poach for three to four minutes. Take the fish poacher or pan off the heat and let it cool. When cool, place in the refrigerator to chill thoroughly—at least three hours.

Carefully remove the cheesecloth-wrapped roll from the pan, and cut away the string and the muslin strips. Just before serving, unwrap the roll, taking care not to break the fish, and cut into ½-inch slices. Arrange the slices on a serving plate.

Mixed Seafood Pâté

Serves 20
Working time: about 45 minutes
Total time: about 3 hours (includes marinating)

Calories **45**
Protein **7g.**
Cholesterol **70g.**
Total fat **1g.**
Saturated fat **1g.**
Sodium **200mg.**

½ lb. smoked cod or haddock
½ lime, juice squeezed, zest grated (optional)
1 cup unsalted fish stock (recipe, page 139), or 1 cup water, plus 2 bay leaves, 6 peppercorns, and 2 tbsp. white wine vinegar
½ lb. cod or haddock, skinned and boned
5 oz. codfish roe
1 tbsp. chopped fresh dill, plus 1 sprig dill for garnish
2 tbsp. anise-flavored liqueur
2 tbsp. plain low-fat yogurt
4 tbsp. sour cream
¼ tsp. cayenne pepper
paprika
ground white pepper
1 tsp. canned green peppercorns, crushed (optional)
2 lime slices for garnish

Skin and coarsely chop the smoked fish into 2-inch pieces. Place the pieces in a shallow, nonreactive dish, pour the lime juice over them, and let them marinate in a cool place for about two hours.

Meanwhile, bring the fish stock or flavored water to a boil in a small saucepan, then simmer the fresh fish gently in the liquid until the flesh flakes easily—three to five minutes.

Remove the fish from the pan with a slotted spoon and set it aside to cool.

Drain the marinade from the smoked fish and flake the flesh. Reserve about one-quarter of the fish, and place the rest in a blender or a food processor. Flake the poached fish, reserve one-quarter of it, and place the rest in the blender.

Add the codfish roe and blend the mixture briefly. Add the dill, anise-flavored liqueur, low-fat yogurt, sour cream, the cayenne pepper, some paprika, and some ground white pepper, as well as the grated lime zest and the crushed peppercorns, if you are using them; blend the mixture until it is smooth. Stir in the reserved fish.

Spoon the mixed seafood pâté into a serving dish. Garnish the pâté with some paprika, the lime slices, and the dill sprig.

SUGGESTED ACCOMPANIMENT: *Melba toast (recipe, page 11).*

Chopped Lamb and Bulgur

KNOWN AS *KIBBEH NAYEH* IN ARAB COUNTRIES, THIS DISH OF RAW MEAT AND BULGUR ORIGINATED IN TURKEY. IT IS ALWAYS MADE WITH VERY LEAN LAMB.

Makes about 30 disks
Working (and total) time: about 20 minutes

Per 3 disks:
Calories **175**
Protein **18g.**
Cholesterol **35mg.**
Total fat **5g.**
Saturated fat **2g.**
Sodium **150mg.**

1 lb. lean lamb for chopping, trimmed of fat
½ lb. fine-grade bulgur
1 large onion, grated
1 tsp. ground cumin
1½ tsp. cayenne pepper
1 tsp. salt
freshly ground black pepper
4 scallions, finely chopped
2 tbsp. finely chopped parsley
small leaves of crisp lettuce

Pass the meat three times through the fine blade of a grinder or chop it finely in a food processor. Put the bulgur into a large bowl, pour boiling water over it, and let it stand for two minutes. Drain the bulgur in a sieve and rinse it under cold running water; scoop up handfuls of bulgur and squeeze out excess water, returning it to the bowl as you proceed.

Combine the chopped meat, onion, cumin, and cayenne pepper in a food processor to make a coarse paste. Add the paste to the bowl of bulgur, season with the salt and some freshly ground black pepper, and knead for at least 10 minutes to mix all the ingredients; add about 2 tablespoons of cold water while kneading to moisten the mixture.

When the paste is smooth, mix in the chopped scallions and parsley. Make about 30 little balls, then flatten these with your thumb into small disks. Serve the lamb and bulgur disks on individual lettuce leaves for eating with the fingers.

Rabbit Terrine

THIS LIGHT, MOIST TERRINE MAY BE SERVED IN SLICES OR
CUT UP AS BITE-SIZE PIECES.

Makes 12 slices
Working time: about 30 minutes
Total time: about 6 hours (includes chilling)

Per slice:
Calories **100**
Protein **12g.**
Cholesterol **40mg.**
Total fat **4g.**
Saturated fat **2g.**
Sodium **120mg.**

1 tbsp. unsalted butter
1 onion, finely chopped
2 tbsp. unbleached all-purpose flour
2 bay leaves
4 cloves
1 cup beer
½ tsp. salt
freshly ground black pepper
1 lb. boned rabbit, finely chopped
6 oz. lean pork loin, finely chopped
1 tsp. honey
1 tbsp. cranberries
watercress leaves, washed and dried

Preheat the oven to 325° F. Line the bottom and sides
of a 2-pound loaf pan with aluminum foil.

Melt the butter in a heavy-bottomed saucepan over
medium heat, add the onion, and cook for one minute,
stirring occasionally. Stir in the flour, bay leaves, cloves,
beer, salt, and some pepper. Bring to a boil, stirring,
and cook for two minutes. Remove the pan from the
heat; discard the bay leaves and cloves, and stir in the
rabbit and pork.

Pour the mixture into the prepared pan and smooth
the top. Cover with a double thickness of aluminum
foil. Set the pan in a larger pan, and pour water into
it until it comes halfway up the sides of the loaf pan.
Bake in the center of the oven until the terrine is firm—
about one and a half hours.

Remove the pan from the water, loosen the foil, and
place a heavy weight on top of the terrine. Chill the
rabbit terrine in the refrigerator for four to five hours
or overnight.

Put the honey into a small saucepan with 1 tablespoon of cold water, bring to a boil, then lower the
heat. Add the cranberries and cook for just one minute
to soften them; do not allow the berries to burst.
Remove the berries with a slotted spoon and place on
paper towels. Let them dry.

To serve, turn the terrine out onto a plate, garnish
with the cranberries and watercress leaves, and cut
into slices or tiny squares.

SUGGESTED ACCOMPANIMENT: *crackers or toast.*

Pork Sticks with Tomato and Fennel Sauce

Makes about 40 sticks
Working time: about 30 minutes
Total time: about 1 hour and 20 minutes

Per stick:
Calories **30**
Protein **2g.**
Cholesterol **30mg.**
Total fat **2g.**
Saturated fat **1g.**
Sodium **30mg.**

1 whole pork loin (about 14 oz.), trimmed of fat
2 tsp. virgin olive oil
½ tsp. fennel seeds, lightly crushed
¼ tsp. salt
freshly ground black pepper
2 medium fennel bulbs (about 12 oz.), feathery tops chopped, bulbs halved
1 thick slice of lemon
Tomato and fennel sauce
2 tbsp. virgin olive oil
1 garlic clove, finely chopped
1 large fennel bulb (about 8 oz.), trimmed and coarsely chopped
½ tsp. fennel seeds, lightly crushed
2 tsp. grated orange zest
4 tbsp. anise-flavored liqueur
freshly ground black pepper
3 medium tomatoes, peeled, seeded (technique, page 76), and chopped
¼ tsp. salt
orange zest, julienned, for garnish

Preheat the oven to 450° F. Brush the pork lightly with the 2 teaspoons of oil and rub with the crushed fennel seeds. Roast the pork for 20 to 25 minutes, then season with the salt and some pepper, cover loosely with foil, and let it cool.

Meanwhile, make the sauce. Heat the oil in a sauté pan and cook the garlic over low heat for a minute or two. Stir in the chopped fennel, fennel seeds, grated orange zest, anise-flavored liqueur, and some pepper. Cover and simmer for 10 minutes. Add the tomatoes and simmer for 10 minutes more; allow to cool. Discard the orange zest, then blend the sauce in a food processor. Add the salt and set aside.

Parboil the fennel bulbs with the lemon slice until the fennel is just tender—about five minutes. Drain, and discard the lemon; refresh the fennel under cold running water and drain well. Cut the fennel into about forty ½-inch cubes.

Unwrap the cooled pork and cut it lengthwise into strips, then slice crosswise to give about forty ¾-inch cubes. Thread cocktail sticks with one piece of fennel and one of pork. Dip the sticks in the chopped fennel tops and arrange them on a serving dish. Serve the sauce separately in a bowl, garnished with the julienned orange zest.

Pork and Cheese Canapés with Apricot Chutney

Makes 36 canapés
Working time: about 20 minutes
Total time: about 12 hours (includes soaking)

Per pork canapé:
Calories **35**
Protein **2g.**
Cholesterol **5mg.**
Total fat **1g.**
Saturated fat **0g.**
Sodium **20mg.**

Per cheese canapé:
Calories **45**
Protein **2g.**
Cholesterol **5mg.**
Total fat **3g.**
Saturated fat **0g.**
Sodium **50mg.**

4½ oz. lean cold roast pork, cubed
36 Melba toasts, approximately 1½ inches square
4 kumquats, thinly sliced, or 72 golden raisins
flat-leaf parsley for garnish
¼ cup low-fat ricotta cheese
Apricot chutney
2 oz. dried apricots, covered with boiling water and soaked for 12 hours
1 tbsp. honey
1 tbsp. cider vinegar
¾-inch piece fresh ginger, peeled and finely chopped
½ tsp. ground cinnamon
⅛ tsp. ground allspice
⅛ tsp. salt

To make the chutney, drain the apricots, and purée them with the honey in a food processor. Add the vinegar, ginger, cinnamon, allspice, and salt, and blend thoroughly. Put the chutney into a bowl or a jar.

Chop the pork in a food processor until it binds together. Add two-thirds of the chutney and blend to form a smooth paste.

Spread the meat and chutney paste over half of the toasts, and garnish each with a slice of kumquat or 2 golden raisins, and a parsley leaf. Spread the ricotta cheese over the remaining toasts, and top each with a ½ teaspoon of the chutney. Arrange the canapés on a serving plate.

EDITOR'S NOTE: *Any excess chutney may be kept in the refrigerator for up to two weeks.*

Vegetable Aspic

TO MAKE A CLEAR VEGETABLE ASPIC, THE BOWLS AND COOKING UTENSILS MUST BE SCRUPULOUSLY CLEAN. HERE, EVERYTHING IS SCALDED TO ENSURE THAT THE LIQUID DOES NOT BECOME CLOUDED BY IMPURITIES.

Makes about 3½ cups
Working time: about 45 minutes
Total time: about 2 hours and 45 minutes

Total recipe:
Calories **410**
Protein **53g.**
Cholesterol **0mg.**
Total fat **trace**
Saturated fat **0g.**
Sodium **1,480mg.**

3 medium carrots, sliced
2 medium leeks, sliced
2 onions, finely chopped
4 celery stalks, sliced
1 small bunch parsley

1 sprig rosemary
1 sprig thyme
4 garlic cloves, unpeeled
½ tsp. salt
8 black peppercorns
6 envelopes (1½ oz.) powdered gelatin
2 eggs, whites only, washed shells reserved
1 tbsp. red wine vinegar

Put the carrots, leeks, onions, celery, parsley, rosemary, thyme, garlic, salt, and peppercorns into a large saucepan with 7 cups of cold water. Bring to a boil, then lower the heat and partially cover the saucepan with a lid. Simmer gently until the liquid is reduced by half—about two hours.

Strain the stock through a fine sieve into a large bowl, and discard the vegetables. Measure the stock and add water, if necessary, to make 3½ cups.

Rinse the saucepan and fill it with cold water. Put a wire whisk, a large sieve, and a large, double-layer square of cheesecloth into the saucepan. Bring the water to a boil. Remove the whisk, sieve, and cheese-cloth from the pan; pour the boiling water into a large bowl to scald it, then pour off the water. Place the sieve over the bowl and line the sieve with the cheesecloth.

Pour the stock into the saucepan, and add the gelatin, egg whites and shells, and vinegar. With the scalded whisk, whisk the stock over medium heat until the egg whites form a thick foam on the surface. Stop whisking, then bring the mixture to a boil so that the foam rises to the top of the saucepan—do not allow it to boil over. Remove the pan from the heat and allow the foam to settle back down. Repeat this process twice more, then allow to stand for five minutes.

Very gently and carefully pour the aspic through the lined sieve, without allowing the foam floating on top of the liquid to break up. Let the aspic drain thoroughly, then allow it to cool. As it cools, the aspic sets to a jellylike consistency.

The aspic may be kept in the refrigerator for a few days, ready to be used when needed. Once set, it can be quickly melted by placing the bowl over a saucepan of hot water.

Asparagus Canapés

Makes 12 canapés
Working time: about 45 minutes
Total time: about 1 hour and 10 minutes
(includes setting)

12 asparagus spears	
3 or 4 thin slices rye bread	
½ sweet red pepper, peeled (technique, page 22), seeded, and deribbed	
1½ tbsp. polyunsaturated margarine	
1 small garlic clove, crushed	
1 tbsp. finely chopped parsley	
⅛ tsp. salt	
freshly ground black pepper	
½ cup vegetable aspic (recipe, left), melted	

Per canapé:
Calories **30**
Protein **1g.**
Cholesterol **0mg.**
Total fat **2g.**
Saturated fat **trace**
Sodium **60mg.**

Trim the asparagus, then carefully peel each spear up to the tip. Cook the spears in boiling water until ten-der—three to four minutes—then drain in a colander and refresh under cold running water. Drain the asparagus thoroughly.

Trim the crusts from the rye bread, then cut the slices into 12 oblongs about 2½ by 1¼ inches.

Trim the asparagus tip to the length of the bread oblongs, then slice each tip in half lengthwise. (Use the stalks for a salad.) Cut the red pepper into thin strips about the same length as the asparagus pieces.

Put the margarine, garlic, parsley, salt, and some pepper into a small bowl. Beat until smooth, then spread a thin layer over the rye bread.

Place two asparagus-tip halves on each piece of bread and drape a strip of red pepper across the asparagus. Put the canapés on a wire rack set over a large tray. Stir the aspic over ice, or refrigerate, until it begins to thicken. Carefully spoon the aspic over the canapés to coat them evenly, then refrigerate until firmly set—about 20 minutes. Keep the canapés refrigerated until just before serving.

Seafood Canapés

Makes 12 canapés
Working time: about 1 hour
Total time: about 2 hours and 30 minutes (includes cooling and setting)

6 oz. haddock fillet	
1 egg white	
⅜ tsp. salt	
¼ cup plain low-fat yogurt	
freshly ground black pepper	
3 or 4 thin slices whole-wheat sandwich bread, toasted	
1 tbsp. polyunsaturated margarine	
½ tsp. tomato paste	
2 tsp. finely chopped basil leaves	
½ cup vegetable aspic (recipe, left)	

Per canapé:
Calories **40**
Protein **2g.**
Cholesterol **30mg.**
Total fat **2g.**
Saturated fat **trace**
Sodium **110mg.**

12 large shrimp, cooked, peeled, and deveined if necessary	
3 tsp. black caviar or lumpfish roe	

Rinse the haddock fillet under cold running water and pat it dry with paper towels. Carefully remove the skin from the haddock, then remove any bones and cut the fish roughly into cubes. Put the haddock into a food processor or a blender with the egg white and ¼ teaspoon of the salt, and blend to a smooth paste. Work the paste through a fine sieve into a bowl to remove coarse sinews. Cover the bowl and refrigerate for 30 minutes.

Meanwhile, grease 12 differently shaped, tiny *petit-fours* molds. Pour enough water into a saucepan to fill it about 1 inch deep, set a steamer in the pan, and bring the water to a boil.

Remove the chilled fish mixture from the refrigerator. Gradually beat in the yogurt, then season with some black pepper. Fill the prepared molds with the fish mousse. Place the molds in the steamer, and cover them closely with a sheet of parchment paper or wax paper; steam until the mousse is firm—one and a half to two minutes. Remove the molds from the steamer and refrigerate until they are quite cold.

Using a 1¾-inch plain round cutter, cut 12 rounds from the toast. Put the margarine, tomato paste, basil, the remaining salt, and some pepper into a bowl, and beat together until smooth. Spread a thin layer of the mixture over each round of toast.

Carefully unmold the haddock mousses. Dip each one, balanced on a fork, in the aspic, and place on a round of toast. Put the canapés on a wire rack placed over a tray and refrigerate until set—about five minutes. Dip the shrimp in the aspic and place one on each canapé. Refrigerate until set—about five minutes.

Stir the remaining aspic over ice, or refrigerate, until it begins to thicken. Carefully spoon the aspic over the canapés to coat them evenly. Immediately, spoon a little caviar or roe onto each one. Refrigerate until firmly set—about 20 minutes. Keep the canapés refrigerated until just before serving.

EDITOR'S NOTE: *The haddock mousses may be made the day before and kept in the refrigerator.*

Duck Canapés

Makes 12 canapés
Working time: about 45 minutes
Total time: about 2 hours and 15 minutes (includes cooling and setting)

Per canapé:
Calories **105**
Protein **8g.**
Cholesterol **35mg.**
Total fat **4g.**
Saturated fat **1g.**
Sodium **80mg.**

1 tbsp. virgin olive oil
1 lb. boned duck breasts, skinned
2 tbsp. unbleached all-purpose flour
½ cup unsalted chicken stock (recipe, page 139)
1 small sweet red pepper, peeled (technique, page 22), seeded, deribbed, and puréed
¼ tsp. salt
ground white pepper
½ cup vegetable aspic (recipe, page 50)
2 tsp. honey
12 thin slices kumquat (optional)
6 cranberries
6 thin slices rye bread
1 tbsp. polyunsaturated margarine

Heat the oil in a small frying pan over medium heat. Place the duck breasts in the pan and lightly brown both sides to sear them. Reduce the heat to low, then place a flat plate on top of the breasts to prevent them from curling up. Cook until the duck is tender and the juices run clear when the meat is pierced with a skewer—20 to 25 minutes; turn the breasts over halfway through cooking. Using a slotted spoon, transfer the duck to a plate; cover with another flat plate and place a heavy weight (about 1 pound) on top. Set the duck aside to cool.

Meanwhile, stir the flour into the duck juices remaining in the pan, then gradually add the stock. Bring to a boil, stirring continuously, until the sauce thickens; then lower the heat and simmer for five minutes, stirring occasionally. Remove the pan from the heat and stir 2 tablespoons of the pepper purée into the sauce—any remaining pepper purée will not be needed. Season the sauce with the salt and some white pepper, then stir in 3 tablespoons of the aspic. Cover the surface of the sauce closely with plastic wrap to prevent a skin from forming, and set it aside to cool.

Meanwhile, heat the honey and 1 tablespoon of cold water together in a small saucepan until they come to a boil, then lower the heat. Add the kumquat slices, if you are using them, and cook for one minute to soften slightly. Using a slotted spoon, carefully lift the slices onto paper towels to drain. Add the cranberries to the remaining syrup and cook for no more than one minute, just long enough to soften them; take care not to let the berries burst. Drain on paper towels, then cut each cranberry in half lengthwise.

Cut the duck breasts horizontally into thin slices. Then, using a 2½-by-1⅜-inch oval cutter, cut out 12 shapes and place them on a wire rack set over a large tray. (If necessary, ends of slices may be placed side by side and then cut into shape—the joins will be concealed by the sauce and garnish.)

When the sauce is just beginning to set, spoon it over the duck ovals. Refrigerate until the sauce is firmly set—10 to 15 minutes.

With a knife, cut out 12 ovals from the rye bread, using the noncutting, slightly larger edge of the cutter as a template. Spread each shape with the margarine.

Carefully lift the coated breasts from the rack and place each one on an oval of rye bread. Place these on a clean rack set over a clean tray. Dip the kumquat slices, if you are using them, and the cranberry halves in the aspic, and arrange them neatly on the duck canapés. Refrigerate until set—about five minutes.

Stir the remaining aspic over ice, or refrigerate, until just beginning to set, then spoon it over each canapé to coat evenly. Refrigerate until firmly set—20 to 30 minutes. Keep the canapés refrigerated until just before serving.

EDITOR'S NOTE: *The duck may be cooked up to one day in advance and kept in the refrigerator until needed.*

Chicken Canapés

Makes 12 canapés
Working time: about 1 hour
Total time: about 2 hours and 30 minutes (includes cooling and setting)

Per canapé:
Calories **100**
Protein **10g.**
Cholesterol **25mg.**
Total fat **4g.**
Saturated fat **1g.**
Sodium **125mg.**

1 lb. boned chicken breasts, skinned
1 small onion, coarsely chopped
1 celery stalk, coarsely chopped
1 small carrot, coarsely chopped
1 sprig parsley
1 bay leaf
⅜ tsp. salt
4 black peppercorns
1 cup unsalted chicken stock (recipe, page 139)
2 tbsp. polyunsaturated margarine
2½ tbsp. unbleached all-purpose flour
2 tbsp. plain low-fat yogurt
½ cup vegetable aspic (recipe, page 50)
3 or 4 thin slices whole-wheat sandwich bread, toasted
1 small garlic clove, crushed
1 tbsp. finely chopped parsley
freshly ground black pepper
½ sweet red pepper, peeled (technique, page 22), seeded, and deribbed
strips of cucumber skin

Put the chicken breasts into a saucepan with the onion, celery, carrot, parsley, bay leaf, ¼ teaspoon of the salt, the peppercorns, and stock. Bring to a boil, then lower the heat and cover the saucepan with a tight-fitting lid. Simmer gently until the chicken breasts are just cooked—five to six minutes. Allow to cool, then remove the chicken breasts from the stock and refrigerate until they are quite cold.

Strain the stock and reserve ½ cup—the rest of the stock will not be needed. Melt 1 tablespoon of the margarine in a saucepan and stir in the flour. Gradually add the reserved stock and bring to a boil, stirring all the time until the sauce thickens. Lower the heat and simmer for four to five minutes, stirring occasionally. Remove from the heat and allow to cool slightly. Whisk the yogurt and 3 tablespoons of the aspic into the sauce. Cover the surface of the sauce closely with plastic wrap to prevent a skin from forming, and chill until the sauce begins to thicken—20 to 30 minutes.

Carefully cut each chicken breast horizontally into ¼-inch-thick slices. Using a 2-inch heart-shaped cutter, cut out 12 hearts from the slices of chicken. (If necessary, ends of slices may be placed side by side and then cut into shape—the joins will be concealed by the sauce and garnish.)

Place the hearts on a wire rack set over a large tray. Spoon the sauce over the hearts and refrigerate until set—about 20 minutes.

Using a 2¼-inch heart-shaped cutter, cut out 12 hearts from the toast. Put the remaining margarine into a small bowl with the garlic, parsley, the remaining salt, and some pepper. Beat together until smooth, then spread a thin layer over each toast heart.

Lift the coated chicken pieces from the rack and put one piece on each toast heart. Place them on a clean rack set over a clean tray.

Using a small aspic cutter, cut out petal shapes from the red pepper and the cucumber skin. Dip the petals in the aspic and place them on the chicken hearts. Refrigerate until set—about five minutes. Stir the remaining aspic over ice, or refrigerate, until it is just beginning to thicken. Carefully spoon the aspic over the canapés to coat them evenly. Refrigerate until firmly set—about 20 minutes. Keep the canapés refrigerated until just before serving.

EDITOR'S NOTE: *The chicken may be cooked up to a day in advance and kept in the refrigerator until needed.*

Egg and Watercress Canapés

Makes 12 canapés
Working time: about 30 minutes
Total time: about 1 hour and 30 minutes (includes cooling and setting)

Per canapé:
Calories **35**
Protein **2g.**
Cholesterol **40mg.**
Total fat **2g.**
Saturated fat **trace**
Sodium **70mg.**

3 eggs
3 or 4 thin slices rye bread
1 tbsp. polyunsaturated margarine
1 tbsp. finely chopped watercress leaves, plus 12 whole watercress leaves
⅛ tsp. salt
freshly ground black pepper
½ cup vegetable aspic (recipe, page 50), melted

Put the eggs into a saucepan and cover with cold water. Bring to a boil, then cook over medium-low heat for 10 minutes. Immediately, pour off the boiling water and cool the eggs under cold running water. Carefully remove the shells.

Using a 1¾-inch plain round cutter, cut 12 rounds from the rye bread. Put the margarine, chopped watercress, salt, and some pepper into a small bowl. Beat until smooth, then spread a thin layer over each round of rye bread.

Using an egg slicer, slice the eggs. Choose the 12 best slices and place one on each round of bread. (Use the remaining slices in a salad.)

Dip each whole watercress leaf in the aspic and place one leaf on each canapé. Put the canapés on a wire rack placed over a large tray and refrigerate until set—about five minutes. Stir the remaining aspic over ice, or refrigerate, until it begins to thicken. Carefully spoon the aspic over the canapés to coat them evenly. Refrigerate until firmly set—about 20 minutes. Keep the canapés refrigerated until just before serving.

2 *Mussels on the half shell coated with a fragrant tomato and fennel relish make an appealing and quickly prepared party dish (recipe, page 76).*

Hot Festive Food

With their enticing aromas and satisfying warmth, hot snacks are among the most eagerly received offerings at any gathering. But to present them when they are most welcome requires careful planning. For the guests' enjoyment, as well as your own convenience, you should aim to stagger the arrival of dishes throughout the party.

Use the period just before the party starts to cook those dishes that have the longest cooking times. Have ready some dishes that are precooked and only need reheating; the anchovy-tomato dip *(page 66)* and the mussels on the half shell *(left)* take well to this treatment. Also prepare for the oven or pan any dishes with brief cooking times, such as the sole roulades *(page 85)* and the veal with an apricot and nut stuffing *(page 96)*. At intervals during the party, cook or reheat such dishes, and bring them out piping hot. If the work load becomes overwhelming, remember that many dishes designed for eating hot are just as good served at room temperature. The cocktail quiches *(page 59)*, spicy chicken wings *(page 87)*, and pissaladière tartlets *(page 71)*, for example, are delicious hot or cold.

The 46 recipes in this chapter contain many party favorites presented in a more healthful guise. Popcorn *(page 57)* is flavored with spices in place of excessive salt. High-fat puff-pastry cases are discarded in favor of lower-fat alternatives such as yeast dough, paper-thin phyllo pastry, and lightly oiled bread shapes. Even the sausage roll, perennially popular but notoriously fatty, is transformed beyond recognition into a slender, crisp blanket of whole-wheat bread enclosing a filling of the leanest pork. Indeed, the whole genre of sausages takes a new lease on life: Gone are the mass-produced cylinders of fatty meat and gristle; they are replaced by light mixtures of lean beef and herbs *(page 98)*, vegetables *(page 72)*, and seafood *(page 86)*.

The new, light dishes demand some unique skills. To help you achieve professional results, the chapter includes step-by-step instructions for such techniques as butterflying a rock shrimp, making tortellini, and shaping triangular samosas.

Plantain Chips

Makes 1 bowl
Working time: about 20 minutes
Total time: about 50 minutes

Total recipe:
Calories **110**
Protein **1g.**
Cholesterol **0mg.**
Total fat **6g.**
Saturated fat **1g.**
Sodium **trace**

4 large green plantains
4 tbsp. safflower oil

Remove both ends of the plantains with a stainless-steel knife. Slit the skin of each plantain lengthwise into quarters, then peel off the strips of skin.

With a lightly oiled knife, slice the plantains as thin as possible. Place the slices in a bowl of salted water for about 30 minutes, then drain them and pat them dry with paper towels.

Heat the oil in a nonstick frying pan and fry the first batch of plantain slices over medium heat, turning once, until they are golden brown—one and a half to two minutes. Cook the remaining slices in the same way. As each batch is cooked, remove the slices from the pan with a slotted spoon and lay them on paper towels to absorb any excess fat. Serve the slices hot, in a lined basket or on a large plate.

Fiery Chickpeas

Serves 14
Working time: about 20 minutes
Total time: about 2 hours and 30 minutes
(includes soaking)

Calories **175**
Protein **7g.**
Cholesterol **0mg.**
Total fat **9g.**
Saturated fat **1g.**
Sodium **40mg.**

1 lb. (2¼ cups) dried chickpeas
6 tbsp. virgin olive oil
1 large garlic clove
1½ tsp. cayenne pepper
¼ tsp. salt

Rinse the chickpeas under cold running water. Put them into a large, heavy-bottomed pan and pour in enough cold water to cover them by about 2 inches. Discard any chickpeas that float to the surface. Cover the pan, leaving the lid ajar, and bring the water to a boil; cook for two minutes. Turn off the heat, cover the pan, and soak the peas for at least one hour. (Alternatively, soak the chickpeas overnight in cold water.)

After soaking the chickpeas, drain them well in a colander. Return them to the pan and pour in enough water to cover them by about 2 inches. Bring the liquid to a simmer and cook the chickpeas over medium-low heat until they are quite tender—45 minutes to one hour. (If they appear to be drying out at any point, pour in more water.) When cooked, drain the peas and allow them to cool.

Dry the chickpeas thoroughly on paper towels or a clean tea towel. Heat the oil in a heavy frying pan until it is shimmering. Toss in the peas, stir them for a few seconds, then add the garlic.

Lower the heat to medium and sauté the chickpeas, stirring and tossing them from time to time, until their skins are golden brown—20 to 25 minutes. If the chickpeas pop and jump, either lower the heat slightly or cover the pan.

Transfer the chickpeas to multiple thicknesses of paper towels and roll them around to remove as much oil as possible. Then, while they are still hot, toss them in the cayenne pepper and salt. Serve the chickpeas warm, to be eaten with the fingers.

Savory Popcorn

Makes 3 bowls
Working time: about 15 minutes
Total time: about 20 minutes

Herb bowl:
Calories **555**
Protein **18g.**
Cholesterol **40mg.**
Total fat **34g.**
Saturated fat **10g.**
Sodium **100mg.**

Spice bowl:
Calories **135**
Protein **3g.**
Cholesterol **0mg.**
Total fat **8g.**
Saturated fat **0g.**
Sodium **10mg.**

Curry bowl:
Calories **70**
Protein **2g.**
Cholesterol **0mg.**
Total fat **trace**
Saturated fat **trace**
Sodium **15mg.**

2 tsp. safflower oil
¾ cup popping corn
Herb flavoring
1 tbsp. unsalted butter
1 garlic clove, crushed
1 tbsp. freshly chopped mixed herbs, such as basil, parsley, and chervil
2 tsp. freshly grated Parmesan cheese
2 tbsp. pumpkin seeds
Spice flavoring
1 tsp. dry mustard
1 tsp. tomato paste
½ tsp. hot red-pepper sauce
1 tbsp. honey
1 tbsp. sesame seeds
Curry flavoring
1 tsp. curry powder
1 tsp. turmeric
1 tsp. fresh lemon juice
1 tbsp. honey
1 tbsp. plain low-fat yogurt

To prepare the herb flavoring, melt the butter in a saucepan, then add the crushed garlic, the mixed herbs, the Parmesan cheese, and the pumpkin seeds. Cook, stirring continuously, for one minute, then set the pan aside.

For the spice flavoring, mix together in another saucepan the mustard, tomato paste, hot red-pepper sauce, and honey. Heat over medium-low heat, stirring, until the mixture comes to a boil, then set aside.

To prepare the curry flavoring, mix together in a third saucepan the curry powder, turmeric, lemon juice, and honey. Heat over medium-low heat, stirring, until the mixture boils. Remove the pan from the heat and stir in the yogurt.

While the flavorings are hot, make the popcorn. Heat the oil in a large, heavy-bottomed saucepan; add the popping corn and cover with a lid. Heat over medium-low heat, shaking the pan, until all the corn has popped—two to three minutes; discard any un-popped corn.

Pour approximately one-third of the popcorn into each of the flavorings and stir until evenly coated. When you stir the popcorn into the spice flavoring, add the sesame seeds at the same time.

Put the popcorn into separate bowls and serve immediately, while it is still warm.

Buckwheat Blinis Topped with Goat Cheese

Makes about 60 blinis
Working time: about 45 minutes
Total time: about 2 hours and 30 minutes
(includes proofing)

Per blini:
Calories **35**
Protein **2g.**
Cholesterol **10mg.**
Total fat **2g.**
Saturated fat **trace**
Sodium **65mg.**

1½ cups skim milk
1 envelope (¼ oz.) active dry yeast
1 cup buckwheat flour
1 cup bread flour
¼ tsp. salt
½ tsp. ground caraway seeds
½ tsp. crushed black or white sesame seeds
2 tsp. honey
½ tbsp. unsalted butter
1 egg, separated
Goat-cheese topping
½ lb. soft goat cheese
1½ tbsp. sesame seeds, toasted
1 tbsp. caraway seeds, toasted
1 tbsp. poppy seeds, toasted
2 tbsp. sunflower seeds, toasted

Warm ¼ cup of the milk slightly and stir in the dry yeast. Allow the yeast mixture to stand until it becomes foamy—about 10 minutes.

Sift the buckwheat flour, the bread flour, and the salt into a mixing bowl, stir in the caraway and sesame seeds, and make a well in the flour mixture. In a small pan over low heat, gently warm the remaining milk with the honey and butter until just hot. Remove from the heat and stir in the yeast mixture. Pour the milk and yeast mixture, together with the egg yolk, into the flour, and blend with a wooden spoon, gradually incorporating the flour until the mixture is smooth. Beat for two minutes more.

Leave the batter in a warm place until it is well risen and bubbly—about one hour. The batter should drop easily from a teaspoon; if it is too stiff, add warm water a little at a time and beat. Whisk the egg white and fold it into the batter.

Heat a large griddle or nonstick frying pan *(box, page 86)* over medium heat until a few drops of cold water dance when sprinkled on the surface. Drop the batter a teaspoon at a time onto the griddle, and use the back of the spoon to spread the batter into rounds about 2 inches in diameter. Cook the blinis until they are covered with bubbles and the undersides are quite dry and golden—one to three minutes. Flip the blinis and cook them until the second sides are lightly browned—about one minute more. Wrap up each batch in a folded cloth napkin, and keep them warm in a low oven while you cook the remaining batter.

To make the topping, beat the cheese to a smooth, even texture that falls easily from a spoon. To serve, drop a half teaspoon of cheese on each blini, and sprinkle each with one type of seed.

Cocktail Quiches

Makes 18 quiches
Working time: about 1 hour
Total time: about 1 hour and 20 minutes

Per spinach quiche:
Calories **140**
Protein **5g.**
Cholesterol **35mg.**
Total fat **9g.**
Saturated fat **3g.**
Sodium **165mg.**

Per asparagus quiche:
Calories **120**
Protein **4g.**
Cholesterol **30mg.**
Total fat **8g.**
Saturated fat **2g.**
Sodium **160mg.**

Per mackerel quiche:
Calories **115**
Protein **6g.**
Cholesterol **35mg.**
Total fat **7g.**
Saturated fat **2g.**
Sodium **230mg.**

1⅓ cups unbleached all-purpose flour
⅜ tsp. salt
6 tbsp. polyunsaturated margarine
1 egg white, lightly beaten
2 eggs
1 cup skim milk
freshly ground black pepper
2 oz. Parmesan cheese,   *finely grated (about ½ cup)*

Spinach filling

1 tbsp. virgin olive oil
½ small onion, finely chopped
⅓ small sweet red pepper, chopped
⅓ small green pepper, chopped
½ lb. spinach, stems removed, washed

Asparagus filling

3 small asparagus spears, trimmed
3-inch piece cucumber, peeled, halved lengthwise,   *and seeded*
1 tbsp. unsalted butter

Mackerel filling

2 oz. smoked mackerel fillet, or other smoked fish fillet,
such as trout, chub, whiting, etc.

To make the dough, sift the flour and ⅛ teaspoon of the salt into a bowl, then rub in the margarine until the mixture resembles fine breadcrumbs. Add the beaten egg white and mix with a wooden spoon to form a dough. Knead the dough on a lightly floured surface until it is smooth.

Roll out the dough; then, using a 4-inch plain round cutter, cut out rounds. Fit the rounds into 2¾-inch fluted tartlet pans. Trim the edges, then reknead and reroll the trimmings. Cut out more rounds and line more pans, continuing until you have lined 18 pans. Place the pans on baking sheets and refrigerate them while you are making the three fillings.

To prepare the spinach filling, heat the oil in a small frying pan, add the onion and peppers, and cook over very low heat until the vegetables are soft but not browned—six to eight minutes.

Meanwhile, bring a small saucepan of water to a boil, plunge the spinach leaves into the water, and bring back to a boil for 30 seconds. Drain the spinach in a colander, then rinse under cold running water to refresh it. Squeeze the spinach dry and chop finely. Put the spinach and the pepper mixture into a small bowl, and set aside.

For the asparagus filling, cut the tips off the asparagus spears and thinly slice the stalks. Cook the asparagus in a little boiling water until tender—two to three minutes. Drain in a colander, then refresh under cold running water. Drain well. Cut the cucumber halves in half again lengthwise, then into thin slices. Heat the butter in a small saucepan, add the cucumber, and cook until it is soft but not browned—three to four minutes. Set the asparagus tips aside, and put the slices and the cucumber into a small bowl.

To prepare the mackerel filling, remove the skin from the mackerel, then flake the flesh and remove the bones. Put the flesh into a small bowl and set it aside.

Preheat the oven to 425° F.

Put the eggs and milk into a bowl, and season with the remaining salt and some pepper. Whisk lightly together, then stir in the Parmesan cheese. Divide the egg mixture equally among the three bowls of filling and mix each one well.

Fill six of the pastry-lined pans with the asparagus mixture, six with the spinach, and six with the mackerel. Cut the reserved asparagus tips in half and place a piece on each asparagus quiche. Bake the quiches in the oven until they are golden brown and the filling is set—20 to 25 minutes. Carefully transfer the quiches from their pans to a serving plate. Serve warm.

Zucchini Soufflés

Makes 40 soufflés
Working time: about 20 minutes
Total time: about 30 minutes

Per soufflé:
Calories **10**
Protein **trace**
Cholesterol **10mg.**
Total fat **trace**
Saturated fat **trace**
Sodium **20mg.**

5 zucchini, each about 7 inches long, ends trimmed
1 tsp. polyunsaturated margarine
2 tbsp. unbleached all-purpose flour
4 tbsp. skim milk
1 egg yolk
1 oz. sharp Cheddar cheese, grated (about 2 tbsp.)
¼ tsp. Dijon mustard
¼ tsp. salt
freshly ground black pepper
2 egg whites

Using a canelle knife or a vegetable peeler, cut away thin, evenly spaced strips of skin from the length of each zucchini to create a crimped effect. Cut each zucchini into eight slices, each about ¾ inch thick. Using a small spoon, scoop out the center of each slice, taking care not to pierce the base.

Preheat the oven to 425° F. Cook the zucchini slices in boiling water until they are bright green and almost tender—about one minute. Drain them well in a sieve, and arrange them on a baking sheet lined with parchment paper.

To prepare the soufflé filling, place the margarine and flour in a small saucepan over low heat, and whisk until the ingredients are well blended. Gradually whisk in the milk, increase the heat to medium, and bring to a boil. Lower the heat and cook for five minutes, still whisking continuously. Remove the saucepan from the heat, and whisk in the egg yolk, cheese, mustard, salt, and some pepper until evenly mixed.

In a clean bowl, whisk the egg whites until they are stiff but not dry. Add the egg white to the cheese sauce, one-third at a time, carefully folding it into the mixture until all the egg white has been incorporated. Place teaspoons of the soufflé mixture into the zucchini containers, filling each to the top.

Bake the soufflés on the top rack of the oven until the soufflé mixture is well risen and golden brown—five to eight minutes. Arrange the zucchini soufflés on a serving plate, and serve hot or warm.

EDITOR'S NOTE: *Variants of this recipe can be made with artichoke bottoms or hearts, mushrooms, or tomato halves in place of the zucchini slices.*

Feta and Phyllo Parcels

Makes 12 parcels
Working time: about 30 minutes
Total time: about 45 minutes

Per parcel:
Calories **75**
Protein **2g.**
Cholesterol **5mg.**
Total fat **6g.**
Saturated fat **1g.**
Sodium **130mg.**

4 sheets phyllo pastry, each about 18 by 12 inches
3 tbsp. virgin olive oil
4 oz. feta cheese, rinsed, patted dry, and cut into 12 pieces
1 tbsp. finely chopped fresh mint

Preheat the oven to 350° F.

Place one sheet of phyllo pastry on a work surface and brush it with a little of the oil. Place a second sheet on top of the first and brush with oil. Turn over the two sheets together and brush the upper surface. (Keep the other two sheets of phyllo pastry covered with a damp cloth to prevent them from becoming brittle.)

Using a saucer about 6 inches in diameter as a template, cut out six disks from the double sheet of oiled phyllo. Place a piece of feta cheese and a little fresh mint in the center of each disk. Gather up the phyllo edges carefully and twist them slightly to make a frill. Transfer the parcels to a baking sheet. Repeat with the remaining phyllo sheets.

Bake the parcels on the lower rack of the oven for five minutes, then lower the temperature to 325° F., and bake until the bottoms and sides are evenly colored—10 to 15 minutes more. Transfer the parcels to a warm serving platter and serve at once.

Potato Canapés

Makes about 30 canapés
Working time: about 20 minutes
Total time: about 30 minutes

Per canapé:
Calories **25**
Protein **1g.**
Cholesterol **5mg.**
Total fat **1g.**
Saturated fat **trace**
Sodium **30mg.**

4 waxy new potatoes (12 oz.), scrubbed and dried
2 tbsp. unsalted butter
2 garlic cloves, crushed
1 tbsp. finely chopped celery leaves
1 tbsp. finely chopped parsley
½ tsp. salt
freshly ground black pepper
4 orange segments, cut into slices, for garnish
Celery topping
2 celery stalks, finely chopped
2 oz. turkey breast meat, chopped
1 tbsp. pine nuts, chopped
1 tsp. finely grated orange zest
1 tsp. Dijon mustard

Preheat the oven to 425° F.

Cut the potatoes into ¼-inch slices and cook them in a saucepan of boiling water until they are almost tender—about one minute. Drain the potato slices well and transfer them to a bowl.

Put the butter, garlic, celery leaves, parsley, salt, and some pepper into the saucepan, and stir until the butter has melted. Pour half of this mixture onto the potato slices and toss well to coat them evenly.

Line a baking sheet with parchment paper. Remove the potatoes from the bowl with a slotted spoon and arrange them, evenly spaced, on the baking sheet. Bake the slices in the oven until they are lightly browned—four to five minutes.

While the potatoes are baking, prepare the topping. Add the celery, turkey, pine nuts, orange zest, and mustard to the remaining garlic butter in the saucepan. Cook the mixture over medium heat for one minute, stirring occasionally. Add a few more gridings of pepper if desired.

Place spoonfuls of the mixture on top of each potato slice, dividing the mixture evenly. Return the potato slices to the top shelf of the oven and bake until the topping has set—about five minutes. Arrange the potato canapés on a serving plate and garnish each with a slice of orange. Serve hot or warm.

EDITOR'S NOTE: *In place of the turkey, you may substitute chicken, veal, or whitefish.*

Curried Vegetable Pancakes with Cilantro-Lime Yogurt

Makes about 30 pancakes
Working (and total) time: about 1 hour

Per pancake:
Calories **25**
Protein **10g.**
Cholesterol **1mg.**
Total fat **1g.**
Saturated fat **trace**
Sodium **40mg.**

½ cup unbleached all-purpose flour
½ cup whole-wheat flour
½ tsp. baking powder
½ tsp. salt
1 tsp. punch puran (optional)
1 tsp. garam masala (glossary, page 140)
1 tsp. ground turmeric
½ tsp. ground cardamom
½ cup plain low-fat yogurt
1 tbsp. grape-seed or safflower oil
1 large sweet potato, peeled and finely diced or grated
¼ lb. celeriac, peeled and finely diced or grated
Cilantro-lime yogurt topping
½ cup plain low-fat yogurt
⅛ tsp. salt
1 tsp. lime juice
½ tsp. freshly grated lime zest
1 small bunch cilantro, chopped

To make the topping, mix together the yogurt, salt, lime juice and zest, and cilantro. Pour the mixture into a serving bowl and chill it in the refrigerator.

To make the batter, first sift the all-purpose and whole-wheat flour, baking powder, and salt into a mixing bowl. Dry-fry the punch puran, if you are using it, in a fairly hot, heavy-bottomed skillet until the mixture smells highly aromatic—about two minutes. Add it to the flour with the garam masala, turmeric, and cardamom, stir, and make a well in the center of the flour. Mix the yogurt with ½ cup of water and pour the mixture into the well with the oil. Blend together, gradually incorporating the dry ingredients into the liquid. Beat lightly but thoroughly until no lumps remain. Stir in the sweet potato and celeriac.

Preheat the oven to 325° F. Set a griddle or frying pan *(box, page 86)* over medium heat until a few drops of water dance when sprinkled on the surface. Drop tablespoons of the batter onto the griddle and use the back of the spoon to spread the batter into rounds. Cook the pancakes, a few at a time, over medium heat until they are lightly browned—four to five minutes. Cut into one pancake to test the tenderness of the vegetables. Transfer the pancakes to a platter, cover them loosely with foil, and put them in the oven while you cook the remaining batter. (If the pancakes stick, wipe the pan with oil before cooking each batch.)

Serve the warm pancakes topped with a teaspoon of the cilantro-lime yogurt.

SUGGESTED ACCOMPANIMENT: *lime pickle or cucumber salad.*

EDITOR'S NOTE: *Punch puran, a mixture of cumin, fennel seed, mustard seed, onion seed, and fenugreek, is available in Asian markets—as are garam masala, turmeric, and cardamom.*

Tricolor Tortellini Filled with Mushrooms

Makes about 60 tortellini
Working (and total) time: about 3 hours and 30 minutes

Per 3 tortellini:
Calories **180**
Protein **8g.**
Cholesterol **15mg.**
Total fat **5g.**
Saturated fat **1g.**
Sodium **95mg.**

⅛ tsp. saffron strands
½ tsp. salt
3 cups bread flour
1 cup fine semolina
2 small eggs, beaten
2 tbsp. tomato paste
2 oz. cooked spinach, drained thoroughly, finely chopped
1 tbsp. virgin olive oil
Mushroom filling
1 tsp. virgin olive oil
2 garlic cloves, crushed
2 oz. dried porcini (cepes), covered with ½ cup hot water and soaked for about 20 minutes
12 oz. large mushrooms, wiped clean and finely chopped
2 sprigs fresh thyme, leaves only
¼ tsp. salt
1 tbsp. Marsala or brandy
¼ tsp. grated nutmeg
freshly ground black pepper
3 tbsp. low-fat ricotta cheese
2 tbsp. parsley, finely chopped
Yogurt dip (optional)
3 garlic cloves, crushed
1 tsp. virgin olive oil
¾ cup plain low-fat yogurt
4 tbsp. parsley, finely chopped
½ tsp. finely grated lemon zest
¼ tsp. salt

To make the dip, sauté the crushed garlic in the oil for five minutes, then transfer the garlic to a bowl. Add the yogurt, parsley, lemon zest, and salt, and blend the mixture with a fork; set aside.

To prepare the filling, put the oil and garlic into a small saucepan, cover, and place over low heat for five minutes. Meanwhile, remove the dried mushrooms from their soaking liquid, rinse them thoroughly, and chop them finely; filter the soaking liquid through a paper coffee filter and reserve 3 tablespoons. In a wide, heavy sauté pan, combine the soaked dried mushrooms with the fresh mushrooms, garlic, thyme, salt, reserved soaking liquid, and Marsala or brandy. Cover the pan and simmer the mixture over low heat for 20 minutes. Then remove the lid, increase the heat, and cook briskly for a few seconds to eliminate excess moisture, stirring continuously.

Transfer the mixture to a bowl, season with the nutmeg and some freshly ground black pepper, and beat in the ricotta and the parsley. Set the filling aside to cool while you make the three pastas.

Grind the saffron strands with one-third of the salt in a mortar and pestle. Put one-third of the flour, one-third of the semolina, one-third of the beaten egg, and the saffron in a food-processor bowl. Using the metal chopping blade, process until fine crumbs are formed—about 30 seconds. Add water—up to 4 tablespoons—a little at a time through the feed tube until the dough forms a ball. Place the dough in a bowl, cover it with plastic wrap, and set it aside.

In the processor, combine half the remaining flour, semolina, salt, and beaten egg to form fine crumbs. Add the tomato paste and process until small lumps are formed. After a few seconds, add water, a little at a time, until the dough forms a ball. Put the dough into a bowl, cover it, and set it aside.

Shaping Tortellini

1 *ADDING THE FILLING. With a 2-inch cookie cutter, stamp circles from a sheet of pasta dough. In the middle of each circle, put a ½ teaspoon of filling. Using a pastry brush or your finger, moisten the circle's edge with water.*

2 *MAKING THE FIRST FOLD. Fold over the circle of dough to form a half-moon containing the filling. To seal in the filling, pinch the moistened edges of the dough together between your thumb and forefinger.*

3 *BENDING THE HALF-MOON INTO SHAPE. Take one end of each half-moon in either hand and curve it gently until its ends are just overlapping. At the same time, fold the sealed margin of the dough back toward the straight edge of the shape to make a groove around the edge. Pinch the ends of the curled half-moon firmly together so that the shape remains curled.*

Combine the remaining flour, semolina, salt, and egg as above. Add the spinach and process until small lumps form. Continue processing, adding water a little at a time if needed, until the dough forms a ball. Transfer the dough to a bowl, cover it, and set it aside.

Divide the ball of saffron dough into quarters, and pass one-quarter at a time through successive settings of a manual pasta extruder, stopping at the next to the last setting; flour the dough whenever it feels sticky. Cover three of the sheets of dough with a damp cloth to prevent them from drying out. Using a 2-inch round cookie cutter, cut as many circles as possible from the remaining pasta sheet. Fill and shape the saffron circles into tortellini *(technique, left)*, and discard the trimmings. Repeat with the remaining sheets of saffron dough. Put the completed tortellini on a floured surface; ensure that they are not touching. Quarter and roll out the other two pasta balls, and assemble tomato and spinach tortellini in the same way.

In a large saucepan, bring 7 cups of lightly salted water to a boil. Gently drop about one-quarter of the tortellini into the water, bring back to a boil, and cook until they rise to the surface—three to five minutes. Remove them from the water with a slotted spoon, then drain well, and brush lightly with the oil. Cook the remaining tortellini in batches in the same way, keeping the cooked tortellini warm in a covered container in a low oven. Thread the tortellini onto skewers or serve them with cocktail sticks. Serve hot, with the yogurt dip, if you wish.

EDITOR'S NOTE: *The pasta dough can be made and rolled out by hand: Add the beaten egg, flavorings, and 2 to 3 tablespoons of water to the flour mixture, and knead it for about five minutes, adding more water if necessary, until the dough has formed a smooth, elastic ball. Allow the dough to rest, covered, for about one hour. When rolling out the dough, keep the surfaces floured so that the pasta does not stick, and roll as quickly as you can; press down quite hard and roll the pasta as thin as possible.*

Baby Potatoes Coated with Herbs and Parmesan

Makes about 30 potatoes
Working (and total) time: about 20 minutes

Per potato:
Calories **65**
Protein **2g.**
Cholesterol **trace**
Total fat **3g.**
Saturated fat **1g.**
Sodium **60mg.**

3 lb. small new potatoes, scrubbed
4 tbsp. virgin olive oil
2 oz. Parmesan cheese, freshly grated (about ½ cup)
fresh dill, chives, parsley, or mint, or any combination of these, chopped
½ tsp. salt
freshly ground black pepper

Boil the potatoes until they are just soft—about 15 minutes—then drain them thoroughly.

Place the olive oil, Parmesan cheese, herbs, and salt in a large bowl with a few generous grindings of pepper. Add the potatoes and toss them until they are well coated with the mixture.

Serve the baby potatoes hot or warm, speared with cocktail sticks.

Anchovy-Tomato Dip

Serves 10
Working (and total) time: about 1 hour

Calories **55**
Protein **3g.**
Cholesterol **trace**
Total fat **2g.**
Saturated fat **trace**
Sodium **155mg.**

7 garlic cloves
1 tbsp. virgin olive oil
4 anchovy fillets, rinsed and drained
1½ lb. plum tomatoes, peeled, seeded (technique, page 76), and coarsely chopped
¾ tsp. powdered dried oregano
1½ tbsp. tomato paste
1½ tbsp. red wine vinegar
1½ tsp. light brown sugar
2½ cups broccoli florets
6 oz. mushrooms
1 tbsp. chopped fresh basil
1 sweet red pepper, seeded, deribbed, and cut into 1-inch squares
1 yellow pepper, seeded, deribbed, and cut into 1-inch squares
3½ cups cauliflower florets

Put the garlic and oil into a heavy-bottomed saucepan, and cook over low heat, crushing the garlic cloves with a wooden spoon as they soften. After about 10 minutes, add the anchovies to the pan and cook for five minutes more, stirring constantly and crushing the anchovies; do not allow the mixture to burn. Add the tomatoes, oregano, tomato paste, vinegar, and sugar, and simmer for 20 to 30 minutes, stirring occasionally.

Meanwhile, pour enough water into a saucepan to fill it 1 inch deep. Set a steamer in the pan and bring the water to a boil. Put the broccoli into the steamer, cover the pan tightly, and steam for just one minute. Remove from the steamer and set aside. Wipe the mushrooms with a clean, damp cloth, cut them into bite-size pieces, and set aside.

Sieve the tomato sauce over a bowl, pressing firmly with a spoon to push through as much pulp as possible. Stir in the basil. Transfer the sauce to a small fondue pot and set over a flame.

Arrange the broccoli, mushrooms, peppers, and cauliflower on a serving platter, and provide fondue forks or long bamboo sticks for spearing the morsels and dipping them into the hot sauce.

EDITOR'S NOTE: *The sauce may be prepared ahead and reheated just before serving; add the basil at the last minute.*

Stuffed Zucchini and Baby Onions

Makes 48 pieces
Working (and total) time: about 1 hour and 10 minutes

Per piece:
Calories **15**
Protein **trace**
Cholesterol **0mg.**
Total fat **1g.**
Saturated fat **trace**
Sodium **25mg.**

12 pearl onions
2 tbsp. virgin olive oil
3 garlic cloves, crushed
1 lb. ripe tomatoes, peeled, seeded (technique, page 76), and chopped
1 tbsp. finely cut fresh basil leaves, or 1 tsp. dried basil
2 tsp. tomato paste
½ tsp. salt
freshly ground black pepper
3 zucchini, each about 6 inches long
1 tbsp. sugar
¼ cup fresh whole-wheat breadcrumbs
1 tsp. dried mixed herbs
½ oz. Parmesan cheese, finely grated (about 2 tbsp.)

Peel the onions and trim the bottoms so that they will stand level. Cut about ¼ inch off the top of each onion, then very carefully scoop out the center with a grapefruit spoon or a sharp knife to leave a hollow case—the walls should be about ¼ inch thick. Set the onions aside.

Finely chop the onion trimmings and centers. Heat 1 tablespoon of the oil in a saucepan, add the chopped onion, and cook over very low heat until the onion is soft but not browned—four to five minutes. Stir in the garlic, tomatoes, and basil. Partially cover the saucepan, and cook until the tomatoes are soft and well reduced to form a thick mixture. Stir in the tomato paste, and season with a little of the salt and some pepper. Pour the tomato mixture into a fine sieve placed over a bowl, and allow excess liquid to drain off while you prepare the zucchini and onions.

Trim the zucchini and cut them in half lengthwise. Season the onions and zucchini with the remaining salt and some pepper.

Heat the remaining oil in a wide, shallow sauté pan or frying pan with a lid. Add the sugar, and heat on medium low until it dissolves and turns a golden caramel color. Reduce the heat to low, add the onions, and turn them in the caramel until they are lightly browned all over. Move the onions to one side of the pan and add the zucchini, placing them cut side down. Cover the pan and cook the vegetables until they are tender but still firm—five to eight minutes.

Preheat the broiler. Fill each onion with a little of the tomato mixture, then spoon the rest neatly down the center of the zucchini. Cut each zucchini half into six equal pieces.

Place the vegetables in the broiler pan. Mix together the breadcrumbs, dried herbs, and Parmesan, and sprinkle the mixture over the stuffed vegetables. Cook under the broiler until golden brown. Serve warm.

EDITOR'S NOTE: *The vegetables may be prepared and filled ahead of time, leaving only the broiling to be done when you are ready to serve them.*

Folding Phyllo Packages

1 *MAKING THE FIRST FOLD. Position a strip of phyllo with a short side toward you. Brush the strip lightly with butter. Place a teaspoon of filling on the phyllo about ¾ inch from the end nearest you. Lift one corner of the strip and fold it over the filling so that the corner meets the opposite long side, creating a triangle.*

2 *MAKING THE SECOND FOLD. Using both hands, lift the triangle of phyllo containing the filling and fold it away from you.*

3 *COMPLETING THE PACKAGE. Continue folding the package alternately across and up the strip until you reach the far end; any short band of phyllo remaining at the far end may be trimmed off or folded around the package.*

Miniature Samosas

Makes 32 samosas
Working (and total) time: about 1 hour and 15 minutes

8 oz. potatoes, peeled and chopped	*Per samosa:*
1 medium carrot, sliced	Calories **25**
¼ oz. dried porcini (cepes), morels, or other wild mushrooms, soaked for 20 minutes in hot water	Protein **1g.** Cholesterol **3mg.**
1 tsp. poppy seeds	Total fat **1g.**
2½ tbsp. unsalted butter	Saturated fat **1g.** Sodium **35mg.**
1 small onion, finely chopped	
2 oz. shelled young fresh or frozen peas	
½-inch piece fresh ginger, finely chopped	
½ tsp. garam masala (glossary, page 140)	
½ tsp. salt	
⅛ tsp. cayenne pepper	
4 sheets phyllo pastry, each about 18 by 12 inches	
cilantro sprigs for garnish	
Cilantro-yogurt dip	
15 cilantro sprigs, leaves only, finely chopped	
1 cup plain low-fat yogurt	
freshly ground black pepper	

Boil the potatoes and carrot separately until they are tender—12 to 15 minutes. Drain and let them cool. Chop the carrot into small dice and coarsely mash the potatoes. Drain and squeeze dry the mushrooms, and chop them finely.

Toast the poppy seeds in a dry, heavy-bottomed skillet until they start to change color, then remove them from the heat.

Melt ½ tablespoon of the butter in a heavy frying pan over medium heat, then fry the onion until it is golden brown. Add the peas, mushrooms, and ginger, and cook for two to three minutes, stirring continuously. Add the potatoes and carrot, and mix well. Remove from the heat, stir in the garam masala, salt, and cayenne pepper, and set the filling aside.

Preheat the oven to 400° F.

Cut each sheet of phyllo into eight strips measuring about 12 by 2¼ inches. Keep the phyllo you are not working on covered with a damp cloth. Melt the remaining butter and lightly brush one side of each strip;

then fold the strips into triangular packages, each enclosing about 1 teaspoon of filling, as demonstrated opposite. Place the phyllo packages on a lightly greased or nonstick baking sheet with the seam sides down. Bake the packages in the oven until they are golden brown—15 to 20 minutes.

To make the dip, mix the cilantro with the yogurt and season with some pepper. Serve the samosas hot, garnished with the cilantro sprigs, accompanied by the cilantro-yogurt dip.

Spinach and Ricotta Calzone

Makes 30 calzone
Working time: about 40 minutes
Total time: about 1 hour and 30 minutes

Per calzone:	
Calories **85**	½ tsp. sugar
Protein **4g.**	2 envelopes (½ oz.) active dry yeast
Cholesterol **10mg.**	4 cups unbleached all-purpose flour
Total fat **2g.**	1 tsp. salt
Saturated fat **1g.**	1 tbsp. virgin olive oil
Sodium **150mg.**	1 egg yolk, beaten with 2 tsp. water

Spinach and ricotta filling

1 lb. spinach, washed, stems removed
4 oz. (about ⅓ cup) low-fat ricotta cheese
½ tsp. grated nutmeg
1 tsp. pesto (glossary, page 140)
¼ tsp. salt
freshly ground black pepper
4 oz. low-fat mozzarella, finely cubed

To make the dough for the calzone, first stir the sugar into 1 cup of tepid water, then add the yeast. Let the yeast mixture stand until it is frothy—10 to 15 minutes. Sift the flour and salt into a large bowl, and make a well in the center. Pour in the yeast liquid and the olive oil, and mix, gradually incorporating all the flour into the liquid. Remove the dough from the bowl and knead until it is silky to the touch—about five minutes. Add a little more flour if the dough is sticky. Put the dough into a lightly oiled bowl, cover with lightly oiled plastic wrap, and leave it in a warm place until the dough has doubled in volume—about 45 minutes.

While the dough is rising, make the filling. Place the spinach with the water still clinging to its leaves in a large saucepan. Cover and steam the spinach over medium heat until it is wilted—two to three minutes. Drain and squeeze out all the water. Put the spinach into a blender or a food processor with the ricotta,

nutmeg, pesto, salt, and some pepper, and blend very briefly. Then stir in the mozzarella.

Preheat the oven to 425° F. When the dough has risen, place it on a work surface and knead it slightly to force out the air. Roll out the dough as thin as possible and cut out 30 circles with a 3-inch pastry cutter. Put about a teaspoon of the filling into the center of each circle, moisten the circumference with a little of the egg yolk and water, then fold over and seal in a semicircle. Brush the tops of each calzone with the remaining egg yolk and water, then make a small incision in each one.

Bake the calzone until they are well risen and golden in color—8 to 10 minutes. Serve warm.

EDITOR'S NOTE: *The dough may be prepared in advance and refrigerated for up to 24 hours.*

Eggplant, Tomato, and Crab Croustades

Makes 12 croustades
Working time: about 30 minutes
Total time: about 35 minutes

Per croustade:
Calories **90**
Protein **4g.**
Cholesterol **10mg.**
Total fat **4g.**
Saturated fat **1g.**
Sodium **80mg.**

12 thin slices white bread
3 tbsp. virgin olive oil
one ½-lb. eggplant, peeled and coarsely chopped
1 garlic clove, finely chopped
2 medium tomatoes, peeled, seeded (technique, page 76), and coarsely chopped
½ lemon, strained juice only
½ tsp. salt
freshly ground black pepper
4 oz. crabmeat, picked over
lemon wedges for garnish

Preheat the oven to 400° F. Using a 3-inch round pastry cutter, cut a circle from each slice of bread. Brush both sides of the bread circles lightly with 2 tablespoons of the oil, and press them firmly into 12 muffin cups or small tart pans. Bake in the oven until the bread is golden and has set into shape—about 10 minutes.

Meanwhile, prepare the filling. Heat the remaining oil in a frying pan over medium heat and sauté the eggplant with the garlic. When the eggplant is well browned, stir in the tomatoes, lemon juice, salt, and some pepper. Increase the heat to evaporate all the juices, then spoon the mixture into the croustade cases. Flake the crabmeat and divide it among the cases.

Cover the crab croustades loosely with a piece of aluminium foil and return the tray to the hot oven for five minutes.

Serve hot, garnished with the lemon wedges.

Pissaladière Tartlets

Makes 24 tartlets
Working time: about 1 hour
Total time: about 1 hour and 45 minutes

Per tartlet:
Calories **70**
Protein **2g.**
Cholesterol **trace**
Total fat **3g.**
Saturated fat **trace**
Sodium **45mg.**

1½ tbsp. virgin olive oil
2 large onions (about 1½ lb.), quartered and thinly sliced
1 large garlic clove, finely chopped
6 anchovy fillets, soaked in skim milk for 30 minutes, rinsed in cold water, and patted dry
12 black olives, pitted and quartered
Tartlet dough
1 envelope (¼ oz.) active dry yeast
2 cups unbleached all-purpose flour
¼ tsp. salt
1½ tbsp. virgin olive oil
1 tsp. chopped fresh rosemary, or ½ tsp. dried rosemary

First, prepare the tartlet dough. Dissolve the yeast in ¼ cup of tepid water and set it aside until it foams—about 10 minutes. Sift the flour and salt into a large bowl, make a well in the center, and pour in the yeast solution. Add 1 tablespoon of the oil, the rosemary, and ¾ cup of tepid water, and mix to make a dough that is soft but not sticky. On a floured work surface,

knead the dough until it is smooth and elastic—approximately five minutes.

Put the remaining ½ tablespoon of oil into a mixing bowl. Form the dough into a ball and put it into the bowl; turn the dough to coat it all over with oil. Cover the bowl with a damp dishtowel and leave the dough in a warm place to rise until it has doubled in size—about one hour.

While the dough rises, prepare the filling. Heat the oil in a large frying pan, and stew the onions and garlic for 40 minutes over low heat, adding a little water if necessary to prevent them from sticking.

Cut each anchovy fillet lengthwise into four strips, then halve the strips by cutting across them.

Preheat the oven to 400° F.

Punch down the dough, then turn it out onto a lightly floured surface and knead briefly. Cut the dough into 24 portions. Roll out each portion into a circle about 2½ inches in diameter, and use the circles to line 2½-inch-diameter tartlet pans.

Fill each dough case with a heaped teaspoon of the onion mixture and smooth the surface. Cross two anchovy strips on each tartlet and add two olive quarters. Place the tartlet pans on a baking sheet, and bake the tartlets until the dough has risen and is lightly golden—about 15 minutes. Serve hot.

Eggplant Sausages

Makes about 40 sausages
Working time: about 1 hour
Total time: about 1 hour and 30 minutes
(includes soaking)

Per sausage:
Calories **35**
Protein **2g.**
Cholesterol **5mg.**
Total fat **2g.**
Saturated fat **1g.**
Sodium **65mg.**

1½ lb. eggplant
½ lb. potatoes, peeled and chopped
1¼ cups fresh breadcrumbs
¼ lb. low-fat cream cheese
1 egg, lightly beaten
2 shallots, finely chopped
2 tsp. tomato paste
1 tbsp. chopped parsley
1 tbsp. chopped fresh rosemary
1 tsp. grated nutmeg
½ tsp. salt
freshly ground black pepper
6 feet natural lamb sausage casing, soaked in acidulated water for 1 hour
1 tsp. safflower oil
2 tsp. honey

Green-peppercorn dip

⅔ cup sour cream
2 tsp. green peppercorns, crushed
2 tbsp. chopped capers
1 tbsp. chopped fresh tarragon
2 tsp. tarragon vinegar

Preheat the oven to 425° F. Cut the eggplant in half lengthwise and place the halves cut side down on a foil-lined baking sheet. Bake them until they are tender—20 to 30 minutes.

Meanwhile, cook the potatoes in boiling water until they are almost tender—three to five minutes. Drain them and set aside.

Remove the cooked eggplant from the oven, but leave the oven on. Scoop the flesh out of the eggplant and discard the skin. In a food processor, purée the eggplant flesh, potatoes, breadcrumbs, and cream cheese. Add the egg, shallots, tomato paste, parsley, rosemary, nutmeg, salt, and some pepper, and process until the mixture is thoroughly blended.

Unravel the lamb sausage casing and cut it in half. Roll one end of a length of casing over the spout of a funnel, and run cold water through it to open it out, then rinse the other length in the same way. Drain the casings. Make up the 1-inch sausages as demonstrated on page 98.

Place the linked sausages on a lightly greased baking sheet and brush them with the safflower oil. Bake the sausages in the oven until they are golden brown—12 to 15 minutes.

Meanwhile, make the dip. Mix together the sour cream, peppercorns, capers, tarragon, and vinegar, and pour the mixture into a serving bowl. Then warm the honey in a small saucepan over low heat.

Allow the cooked sausages to cool for two to three minutes before cutting through the links with kitchen scissors. Brush them with the warmed honey and arrange them on a serving dish. Serve hot with the green-peppercorn dip.

EDITOR'S NOTE: *Natural sausage casings—the cleansed intestines of lamb, pig, or cow—can be ordered from your butcher or from specialty suppliers. Use lamb casings for small sausages, as shown here.*

Sigara Borek with Asparagus and Parmesan

BOREK IS A TURKISH WORD FOR A PASTRY-WRAPPED DISH;
SIGARA IS A CIGARETTE.

Makes 12 *sigara*
Working time: about 15 minutes
Total time: about 30 minutes

Per sigara:
Calories **20**
Protein **1g.**
Cholesterol **trace**
Total fat **1g.**
Saturated fat **trace**
Sodium **15mg.**

12 asparagus spears, trimmed and peeled
2 sheets phyllo pastry, each about 18 by 12 inches
3 tsp. freshly grated Parmesan cheese
freshly ground black pepper
½ tbsp. virgin olive oil

Trim the asparagus spears to a length of about 4 inches, discarding any excess stem. Plunge the asparagus into boiling water and cook it for three minutes, then drain it in a colander and refresh under cold running water. Drain the asparagus thoroughly and pat it dry with paper towels.

Preheat the oven to 400° F.

Lay out the sheets of phyllo pastry on a lightly floured board. Cut each sheet in half lengthwise, then cut crosswise three times to make 12 squares about 6 by 6 inches. Sprinkle the phyllo squares evenly with the Parmesan cheese.

Cover the phyllo squares with a damp cloth to prevent them from drying out. Taking one phyllo square at a time, lay an asparagus tip on each square, about 1 inch in from one edge, and sprinkle with some black pepper. Fold the edge over the asparagus, then fold in the two adjacent sides at a slight angle, so that the side of the pastry opposite the spear is narrower. Roll up the spear into a neat cigarette shape and brush with a little of the oil. Make the remaining asparagus rolls in the same manner.

Bake the *sigara* in the oven for 10 to 15 minutes, turning once so that they brown evenly. Serve hot.

Butterflying a Rock Shrimp

1 CUTTING THE UNDERSHELL. Remove and discard the head, and gently pull off the legs. Using small kitchen scissors, cut the undershell of the shrimp along its length.

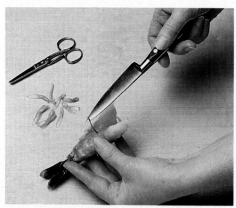

2 SLITTING THE SHRIMP. Using a sharp knife, slit open the shrimp; cut right through the shrimp to its shell without splitting the shell. Remove the intestinal tract running down the back of the shrimp and discard.

3 OPENING OUT THE SHRIMP. Lay the shrimp on the work surface, cut side down. Press hard along the spine of the shell until it cracks. Or, slit the shrimp and shell lengthwise, leaving ½ inch intact in the center of the spine, and push the cut ends apart for a full butterfly effect.

Ginger-Spiced Rock Shrimp

Makes 12 shrimp
Working time: about 30 minutes
Total time: about 2 hours and 30 minutes
(includes marinating)

Per shrimp:
Calories **30**
Protein **3g.**
Cholesterol **20mg.**
Total fat **2g.**
Saturated fat **trace**
Sodium **30mg.**

12 raw rock shrimp, deveined and butterflied (technique, left), or 12 large shrimp, butterflied with the shell on
4 tbsp. low-sodium soy sauce
2 tsp. fresh lemon or lime juice
2 tsp. honey
1-inch piece fresh ginger, peeled and finely chopped, or the juice extracted with a garlic press
1 garlic clove, finely chopped
½ tsp. five-spice powder
1 tbsp. light sesame oil
lettuce leaves, washed, dried, and shredded, for garnish
lemon wedges for garnish (optional)

Combine the soy sauce, citrus juice, honey, ginger, garlic, and five-spice powder in a wide, shallow, non-reactive dish. Place the butterflied shrimp in this mixture, flesh side down, and let them marinate in a cool place for two hours.

Preheat the broiler.

Brush a wide, flameproof pan with 1 teaspoon of the oil. Reserving the marinade, place the shrimp, flesh side down, in the pan. Brush the shells of the shrimp with the remaining oil and broil, turning once, until the shells turn pink and the flesh is no longer translucent—three to five minutes.

Meanwhile, reduce the reserved marinade in a small saucepan over high heat until only 1 tablespoon remains. Brush this glaze over both sides of the shrimp. Serve immediately on a bed of shredded lettuce, accompanied by the lemon wedges, if you wish.

Mussels on the Half Shell

Makes 20 mussels
Working (and total) time: 30 minutes

Per mussel:
Calories **25**
Protein **4g.**
Cholesterol **10mg.**
Total fat **1g.**
Saturated fat **trace**
Sodium **70mg.**

20 mussels (about 1 lb.), scrubbed and debearded
1 lemon, cut into wedges
Tomato and fennel relish
2 tsp. virgin olive oil
2 oz. (about ⅓ cup) finely chopped fennel
2 medium tomatoes, peeled, seeded (technique, right), and chopped
½ tsp. sherry vinegar
1 tsp. tomato paste
1 garlic clove, crushed
¼ tsp. salt
freshly ground black pepper
2 tbsp. finely chopped parsley

Pour 4 tablespoons of water into a large pan. Add the mussels, cover the pan, and bring the water to a boil. Steam the mussels until their shells open—four to five minutes. Discard any mussels that remain closed.

Remove the top shell from each mussel and discard it. Using your fingers or a spoon, sever the connective tissue that attaches the mussel to the bottom shell. Return the mussels to their half shells and place them in an ovenproof serving dish.

Preheat the oven to 375° F.

To make the tomato and fennel relish, first pour the oil into a heavy-bottomed saucepan and sauté the fennel over medium heat until it is fairly soft—about five minutes. Add the tomatoes, vinegar, tomato paste, garlic, salt, and some freshly ground black pepper, and simmer until the mixture is well reduced—about 10 minutes. Stir in the parsley.

Spoon a little of the relish onto each half shell. Cover the dish with aluminum foil, and put it in the oven for about five minutes to allow the mussels and relish to warm through. Serve immediately, garnished with the lemon wedges.

Peeling and Seeding a Tomato

1 *PEELING THE TOMATO. Core the tomato by cutting a conical plug from its stem end. Cut a shallow cross in the base. Immerse the tomato in boiling water for 10 to 30 seconds, then plunge it into cold water. When the tomato has cooled, peel the skin away from the cross in sections.*

2 *SEEDING THE TOMATO. Halve the peeled tomato. Gently squeeze one of the halves, forcing out its seeds and juice. Rotate the tomato 90 degrees and squeeze once more. Dislodge any seeds from the inner chambers. Repeat the process with the other half.*

Red-Hot Monkfish

Makes about 50 bite-size pieces
Working time: about 25 minutes
Total time: about 1 hour and 10 minutes

Per piece:
Calories **25**
Protein **3g.**
Cholesterol **10mg.**
Total fat **1g.**
Saturated fat **trace**
Sodium **20mg.**

6 medium ripe tomatoes, coarsely chopped, or 28 oz. canned tomatoes, drained
2½ tbsp. virgin olive oil
1 small onion, finely chopped
2 garlic cloves, crushed
1 small sweet green pepper, seeded, deribbed, and finely chopped
1 small fresh green chili pepper, seeded and finely chopped (cautionary note, page 18)
⅛ tsp. chili powder
1 tsp. sugar
1 tsp. Dijon mustard
1 tsp. fresh lemon juice
¼ tsp. salt
freshly ground black pepper
2¼ lb. filleted and skinned monkfish

Purée the tomatoes in a food processor or a blender. Press the purée through a sieve into a bowl. Discard the seeds and skin remaining in the sieve. Set aside.

Heat ½ tablespoon of the oil in a heavy-bottomed saucepan, and gently sweat the onion until it is soft but not colored. Add the garlic and sweet green pepper, stir for a minute or two, then add the tomato purée, chili, chili powder, sugar, mustard, and lemon juice.

Bring to a vigorous boil, then lower the heat and maintain a light boil until the sauce has reduced to about 1½ cups—about 40 minutes. Add the salt and some black pepper. Set aside.

While the sauce is reducing, trim the monkfish of any loose membrane and cut it into about fifty 1-inch cubes. Heat 1 tablespoon of the oil in a large sauté pan and cook half of the fish pieces for two to three minutes. Using a slotted spoon, transfer the fish to the sauce. Clean the pan, add the remaining oil, and cook the remaining fish pieces in the same way. Transfer the fish to the sauce and heat through.

Pour a little sauce onto a warm serving dish. Arrange the monkfish on top and then pour any remaining sauce over the fish.

Serve the monkfish hot with cocktail sticks to spear the pieces.

Scallop and Lime Puffs

Makes 16 puffs
Working time: about 40 minutes
Total time: about 1 hour and 20 minutes

Per puff:
Calories **80**
Protein **6g.**
Cholesterol **45mg.**
Total fat **4g.**
Saturated fat **2g.**
Sodium **105mg.**

12 oz. sea scallops, bright white connective tissue removed, rinsed and cut into ¼-inch dice
1½ tsp. cornstarch
1½ tbsp. fresh lime juice, plus ¼ tsp. grated lime zest
1½ tbsp. finely chopped parsley
¼ tsp. salt
freshly ground black pepper
3 tbsp. sour cream
Chou-puff dough
4 tbsp. unsalted butter
¼ tsp. salt
⅔ cup unbleached all-purpose flour
cayenne pepper
2 eggs

Preheat the oven to 425° F. Line a baking sheet with foil or parchment paper. To make the dough, put the butter, salt, and ½ cup of water into a pan, and set over low heat to melt the butter without evaporating any water. Then bring the butter mixture to a boil, remove from the heat, and add the flour and some cayenne, stirring continuously with a wooden spoon. Return the pan to low heat and cook until the mixture forms a ball in the center of the pan. Remove from the heat, let the dough cool for a few minutes, then add the eggs one at a time, mixing after each addition.

Using a pastry bag with a ½-inch plain tip, make 16 mounds on the baking sheet, spaced apart. Alternatively, use a teaspoon to make the shapes. Flatten any ripples or peaks with a wet teaspoon or finger.

Bake the puffs until they are well risen and golden on the sides as well as on top—20 to 25 minutes. Remove the puffs from the oven and pierce each with a pointed knife to let the steam escape, then return them to the oven for four to five minutes to dry out completely. Transfer the puffs to a wire rack to cool.

To make the filling, sprinkle the scallops with the cornstarch, turning and mixing to coat them evenly. Heat a dry, nonstick pan over high heat, add the scallops, and stirring all the time, sear them until they begin to color—about one minute. Lower the heat, add the lime juice and zest, parsley, salt, some pepper, and the sour cream to the pan, and continue to cook, stirring, until the juices thicken—about two minutes.

Fill the puffs just before serving. Warm them in a 350° F. oven, then slice off the top third of each. Spoon the filling into the puffs, replace the tops, and serve.

EDITOR'S NOTE: *The puffs may be prepared in advance and stored in an airtight container for up to five days before being warmed and filled. Alternatively, they can be frozen and then thawed in the oven as they are needed.*

Two-Salmon Won Tons

Makes 16 won tons
Working time: about 20 minutes
Total time: about 1 hour (includes marinating)

Per won ton:
Calories **55**
Protein **3g.**
Cholesterol **10mg.**
Total fat **2g.**
Saturated fat **trace**
Sodium **85mg.**

6 oz. fresh salmon steaks
2 oz. smoked salmon, finely chopped
1 tbsp. fresh lemon juice
1 tsp. finely chopped fresh dill
freshly ground black pepper
16 won-ton wrappers

Skin the fresh salmon and remove all bones; run your fingers over the flesh to find the smaller bones, and remove these with tweezers. Finely chop the flesh, and mix it together with the smoked salmon, lemon juice, dill, and some black pepper. Let it marinate at room temperature for 30 minutes to one hour.

Place about a teaspoon of the salmon mixture in the center of each won-ton wrapper. Dip your fingertips in water and moisten the edges of each wrapper, then bring the four corners together to meet in the center, and press the edges together.

Place the won tons in a bamboo or lightly oiled stainless-steel steamer, cover, and steam over boiling water until the wrappers become translucent—two to five minutes. Serve immediately.

EDITOR'S NOTE: *If won-ton wrappers are not available, you can make your own. Mix 1 egg with 4 tablespoons of water and knead with 2 cups of sifted flour for 5 to 10 minutes. Divide the dough in half and roll out each half into a 14-inch square. Trim the edges and cut each square into 16 equal pieces. The wrappers not used for this recipe may be kept in the refrigerator for up to two days or frozen.*

Sesame Shrimp Toasts

Makes 48 toasts
Working time: about 45 minutes
Total time: about 1 hour

Per toast:
Calories **15**
Protein **1g.**
Cholesterol **5mg.**
Total fat **trace**
Saturated fat **trace**
Sodium **25mg.**

1 tsp. fresh lemon juice
4 oz. cooked, peeled rock shrimp or large shrimp, finely chopped
6 oz. sole fillets or other white-fleshed fish
2 tsp. dry vermouth
1 egg white
¼ tsp. salt
3 tbsp. sour cream
3 tbsp. finely chopped scallions
¼ tsp. cayenne pepper
6 thin slices white bread, trimmed to 3½-inch squares
4 tsp. sesame seeds
lettuce leaves for garnish

Add the lemon juice to the chopped shrimp and set the mixture aside. In a food processor, purée the fish with the vermouth, egg white, and salt. Transfer the mixture from the processor to a bowl and set this in a larger bowl containing ice. Beat in the sour cream. Gently stir in the scallions, cayenne pepper, and shrimp. Preheat the oven to 400° F.

Toast the bread until it is light brown. Spread the shrimp topping over the toast and cover with an even sprinkling of the sesame seeds. Cut each slice of toast into quarters, then cut each quarter diagonally into two triangles. Place the triangles on the baking sheet and bake them in the oven until they are golden brown—15 to 20 minutes. Serve them warm on a bed of lettuce leaves.

Goujonettes with Dill and Gherkin Dip

Serves 10
Working time: about 20 minutes
Total time: about 30 minutes

Calories **95**
Protein **9g.**
Cholesterol **40mg.**
Total fat **4g.**
Saturated fat **3g.**
Sodium **65mg.**

1 cup rolled oats
1 egg white
1 tsp. fresh lemon juice
1 tbsp. whole-wheat flour
¼ tsp. salt
freshly ground black pepper
12 oz. sole, turbot, or halibut fillets, skinned

Dill and gherkin dip

½ cup sour cream
½ cup plain low-fat yogurt
2 baby gherkins, finely chopped
1 tsp. finely chopped fresh dill
1 lemon, grated zest only
freshly ground black pepper

dill sprig for garnish

Preheat the oven to 425° F. Put the rolled oats on a baking sheet, and toast them in the oven until golden brown—10 to 15 minutes—stirring once or twice to be sure that the oats do not burn. Remove them from the oven and allow to cool.

To prepare the dip, mix the sour cream, yogurt, gherkins, dill, lemon zest, and some pepper. Transfer the dip to a serving bowl and garnish with the dill sprig.

Lightly whisk together the egg white and lemon juice; mix the oats with the flour, salt, and some pepper. Cut the fish fillets into strips about 3 by ½ inches. Dip the strips in the egg white, shake off the excess, then roll them in the oat mixture, coating them evenly. Place the strips on a nonstick baking sheet, and cook them in the oven until the fish is tender and the outside lightly browned—three to five minutes. Serve the goujonettes hot, accompanied by the dip.

Monkfish and Ham Rolls

Makes 18 rolls
Working time: about 15 minutes
Total time: about 45 minutes (includes marinating)

Per roll:	
Calories **70**	
Protein **6g.**	
Cholesterol **25mg.**	
Total fat **5g.**	
Saturated fat **2g.**	
Sodium **110mg.**	

1 lb. trimmed, skinned, and boned monkfish or halibut
½ tsp. finely chopped fresh thyme
1 bay leaf, broken
freshly ground black pepper
1 lemon, juice only
18 thin 1-by-4-inch strips lean ham

Cut the fish into 18 cubes, and put them into a bowl with the thyme, bay leaf, some pepper, and the lemon juice. Turn the cubes to coat them well, and let them marinate at room temperature for at least 30 minutes.

Meanwhile, soak 18 short wooden cocktail sticks in cold water for 10 minutes to prevent them from scorching under the broiler.

Preheat the broiler. Discard the pieces of bay leaf from the fish marinade. Wrap each cube of fish with a piece of ham, and thread onto a stick; ensure that the skewers pierce through the overlapping ends of ham to hold them together.

Broil the rolls 5 to 6 inches from the heat for four to five minutes, turning once. Serve immediately.

Halibut Kievski

IN THIS VARIATION OF A TRADITIONAL RUSSIAN SNACK,
FISH INSTEAD OF MEAT IS WRAPPED AROUND
LIGHTLY BUTTERED PEAS.

Makes 24 *kievski*
Working time: about 15 minutes
Total time: about 1 hour and 20 minutes
(includes chilling)

Per kievski:
Calories **20**
Protein **3g.**
Cholesterol **10mg.**
Total fat **1g.**
Saturated fat **trace**
Sodium **25mg.**

10 oz. skinned and boned halibut or haddock, finely chopped
½ tsp. very finely grated lemon zest
⅛ tsp. salt
ground white pepper
1½ oz. shelled fresh peas or frozen peas, thawed
½ tbsp. unsalted butter
24 snow peas (about 4 oz.), strings removed

In a food processor, combine the halibut or haddock with the lemon zest, salt, and some white pepper until it forms a coarse paste. Chill the paste in the refrigerator for at least one hour.

If you are using fresh peas, parboil them until they are just tender—three to four minutes. Drain them, refresh under cold running water, and drain again. (Frozen peas do not need parboiling.) Melt the butter in a small, heavy-bottomed saucepan, remove from the heat, and toss the peas in the butter.

Divide the paste into 24 portions. Roll a portion into a ball, then flatten it in the palm of your hand to form a 3-inch-diameter disk. Place a few peas in the center of the disk, then draw up the sides of the disk to form a ball around the peas. Repeat until all the paste and peas have been used. Wrap a snow pea around each ball and secure it with a cocktail stick.

Pour enough water into a saucepan to fill it about 1 inch deep. Set a lightly oiled stainless-steel steamer in the pan and bring the water to a boil. Put the balls into the steamer, cover the pan, and steam for five minutes. Serve immediately.

Pastry Crescents with a Fish Filling

Makes about 40 crescents
Working time: about 1 hour
Total time: about 2 hours and 20 minutes
(includes proofing)

Per crescent:
Calories **90**
Protein **4g.**
Cholesterol **20mg.**
Total fat **4g.**
Saturated fat **2g.**
Sodium **40mg.**

1 cup skim milk
2 envelopes (½ oz.) active dry yeast
4¾ cups unbleached all-purpose flour
½ tsp. salt
5 tbsp. unsalted butter, melted
1 egg, plus a little beaten egg for glazing
2 tbsp. caraway seeds for garnish
Fish filling
½ tsp. unsalted butter
1 shallot or small onion, finely chopped
1 cup fish stock (recipe, page 139)
8 oz. herring or cod fillet
8 oz. salmon fillet
2 tbsp. finely chopped fresh dill

Warm the milk, sprinkle the yeast over it, and let stand for 10 minutes. Sift the flour with the salt, make a well in the center, and beat in the butter, yeast mixture, and egg, using a wooden spoon. Turn the dough onto a floured surface and knead until the dough feels elastic—about 10 minutes. Cover the dough with plastic wrap and set it aside in a warm, draft-free place until it doubles in volume—one to one and a half hours.

Meanwhile, prepare the filling. Heat the butter in a frying pan over low heat; add the shallot and sauté for 10 minutes. Bring the stock to a boil in a saucepan, add the herring or cod and salmon, and poach over low heat until the fish is just cooked through—about three minutes. Remove the fish from the pan with a slotted spoon, skin it, and flake the flesh. Mix the fish and the dill into the shallot, and set aside to cool.

Punch down the yeast dough and knead it briefly. Divide the dough in half, and roll out the first half on a floured surface to form a rectangle approximately 16 by 11 inches. Using a 2½-inch round pastry cutter or the rim of a glass, cut out about 20 circles from the dough. Place a small amount of the filling in the center of each circle; wet the edges of the circles and bring the two halves together to form a semicircle with the filling inside. Press to seal the edges, and bend the semicircles to form crescents. Repeat the rolling, cutting, and filling procedure with the remaining dough. Dough trimmings can be rekneaded and used to make more crescents.

Brush the beaten egg lightly over the crescents. Sprinkle the caraway seeds over the crescents, and space the parcels on lightly greased baking sheets, ensuring that they do not touch. Let them rise while the oven heats to 400° F. Place the crescents in the oven and bake until they are golden brown—10 to 12 minutes. Serve warm.

Sole Roulades

Makes 24 roulades
Working time: about 35 minutes
Total time: about 45 minutes

Per roulade:	*2 lemon sole or Dover sole (about 12 oz.*
Calories **40**	*each), cut into 8 fillets*
Protein **6g.**	*and skinned*
Cholesterol **20mg.**	*12 large leaves Nappa cabbage*
Total fat **1g.**	*lemon slices for garnish*
Saturated fat **trace**	**Spicy rice filling**
Sodium **45mg.**	*⅓ cup long-grain brown rice*
	¼ tsp. salt
	2 oz. mushrooms, chopped
	2 tomatoes, peeled, seeded (technique, page 76),
	and chopped
	2 tbsp. cream of coconut
	½ tsp. curry powder
	1 tsp. freshly grated ginger

To prepare the filling, add the rice and salt to ¾ cup of water. Bring to a boil in a tightly covered saucepan, then lower the heat, and simmer until the rice is tender and all of the water is absorbed—about 20 minutes. Stir the mushrooms, tomatoes, coconut, curry pow-

der, and ginger into the rice. Mix well and set aside.

Preheat the oven to 400° F. Soak 24 cocktail sticks in water for about 10 minutes to prevent them from scorching in the oven. Line a baking sheet with parchment paper.

Blanch the Nappa cabbage in boiling water for 15 seconds. Drain and refresh it under cold running water, then drain again thoroughly. Cut each leaf lengthwise into two, removing and discarding the stem. Fold each cabbage piece to form a strip about 6 inches long by ¾ inch wide. Divide the rice filling into 24 portions and cover each leaf strip evenly with one portion.

Using a sharp knife, cut each sole fillet into three strips about ¾ inch wide. Place a strip of sole on each rice-topped leaf. Roll up the leaf neatly and secure with a cocktail stick.

Place the rolls on the prepared baking sheet, and bake until the fish is tender and the leaves are still bright green—five to six minutes.

Serve warm, garnished with the lemon slices.

Seafood Sausages

Makes 30 sausages
Working (and total) time: about 30 minutes

Per sausage:	
Calories **25**	*3 oz. sole or flounder fillet, skinned*
Protein **2g.**	*6 oz. monkfish fillet*
Cholesterol **10mg.**	*4 oz. salmon fillet*
Total fat **2g.**	*1 egg white*
Saturated fat **trace**	*1 tsp. green peppercorns, coarsely crushed*
Sodium **65mg.**	*¼ tsp. grated lemon zest*
	1 tsp. salt
	2 tbsp. virgin olive oil
	lemon slices or wedges for garnish

Coarsely chop the sole or flounder, monkfish, and half of the salmon. In a food processor, process the chopped fish for a few seconds, then add the egg white and process until the mixture just becomes pastelike. Finely chop the remaining salmon, and add it to the fish paste along with the peppercorns, lemon zest, and salt.

Divide the fish paste into 30 walnut-size portions and roll each piece into a sausage shape. Heat the oil in a heavy-bottomed frying pan over medium heat until it is hot but not smoking. Fry the sausages, turning them all the time, until they are well browned—one and a half to two minutes. Serve garnished with slices or wedges of lemon.

Oiling Griddles and Frying Pans

While the higher fat content of traditional recipes allows you to cook on the well-seasoned surface of a griddle or a frying pan without using any additional fat, the low-fat recipes in this book often require a slightly different approach to guard against sticking.

A nonstick griddle or frying pan that has been maintained according to the manufacturer's instructions need not be oiled. However, if either is beginning to show signs of wear—particularly scratches—it is a good idea to coat the surface with a film of oil.

Pour ¼ teaspoon of safflower oil onto the griddle or into the frying pan, and rub it all over the bottom with a paper towel. Do not discard the towel; it will have absorbed enough of the safflower oil to allow you to coat the surface several times as needed during the cooking process.

A well-seasoned, heavy griddle or frying pan that does not have a nonstick surface should be treated in the same way, but with 1 teaspoon of oil instead of ¼ teaspoon. In both cases, most of the oil will be retained by the towel and will thus have little effect on the final calorie count.

Spicy Chicken Wings

Makes 24 pieces
Working time: about 30 minutes
Total time: about 5 hours (includes marinating)

Per piece:
Calories **15**
Protein **2g.**
Cholesterol **10g.**
Total fat **trace**
Saturated fat **trace**
Sodium **45mg.**

12 chicken wings
1 cup plain low-fat yogurt
1 tbsp. fresh lemon juice
1 tbsp. honey
1-inch piece fresh ginger, grated
1 tsp. ground turmeric
¾ tsp. each ground coriander, cumin, and lemon grass
½ tsp. salt
curly endive or lettuce for garnish

Cut off the chicken-wing tips, and either discard them or reserve them for making stock. Separate each wing into two at the joint, and trim off loose skin with scissors or a sharp knife.

Combine the yogurt, lemon juice, honey, ginger, turmeric, coriander, cumin, lemon grass, and salt, and spread the mixture over the chicken pieces. Let the chicken marinate in a cool place for at least four hours, preferably overnight. Preheat the oven to 450° F.

Remove the chicken pieces from the marinade, and arrange them in a baking dish or an ovenproof casserole. Bake the chicken in the oven for about 15 minutes. Serve slightly cooled, for ease of handling, on a bed of curly endive or a chiffonade of lettuce.

EDITOR'S NOTE: *The chicken pieces may also be cooked under a hot broiler, turning them at least once, until they are well browned—about 15 minutes.*

Aromatic Chicken Kofta

Makes 30 kofta
Working time: about 45 minutes
Total time: about 1 hour

Per kofta:
Calories **20**
Protein **2g.**
Cholesterol **5mg.**
Total fat **1g.**
Saturated fat **trace**
Sodium **30mg.**

⅓ cup bulgur
12 cardamom pods, seeds only
½ lb. boneless chicken breast, skinned and chopped
1 tsp. ground coriander
½ tsp. ground cumin
6 tbsp. mint, finely chopped
1 garlic clove, crushed
½ tsp. salt
freshly ground black pepper
2 tsp. virgin olive oil
lemon and lime wedges for garnish

Put the bulgur into a small saucepan and add water to cover the bulgur by about ½ inch. Bring to a boil, then cover the pan, and simmer until the bulgur is soft and all the water has been absorbed—about 15 minutes. Set aside to cool.

Set a heavy-bottomed skillet over high heat, add the cardamom seeds, and cook until they start to pop—about one minute. Finely grind the seeds, using a mortar and pestle or a rolling pin.

Preheat the broiler.

In a food processor, combine the chicken, cardamom seeds, coriander, cumin, mint, garlic, salt, and some pepper for a few seconds to form a paste. Add the chicken paste to the bulgur and mix together, then form the mixture into 30 small balls. Brush the balls with the oil, and broil 5 to 6 inches from the heat, turning frequently, until they are crisp and golden—four to five minutes. Serve the kofta hot, accompanied by the lemon and lime wedges.

SUGGESTED ACCOMPANIMENT: *pita bread.*

Miniature Spring Rolls

Makes 32 spring rolls
Working (and total) time: about 1 hour and 30 minutes

Per spring roll:
Calories **25**
Protein **2g.**
Cholesterol **10mg.**
Total fat **1g.**
Saturated fat **0g.**
Sodium **30mg.**

1½ tsp. cornstarch
1 tsp. dry sherry or sake
½ tsp. salt
ground white pepper
¼ lb. chicken breast meat, cut into fine strips
¼ oz. cloud-ear mushrooms, covered with very hot water and soaked for 20 minutes, or 2 oz. fresh shiitake mushrooms
1 egg
2 tbsp. safflower oil
1 garlic clove, finely chopped
½-inch piece fresh ginger, finely chopped
3 oz. (about ¾ cup) bean sprouts
1 small green pepper, seeded, deribbed, and finely shredded
1 small carrot, finely shredded
8 sheets phyllo pastry, each about 18 by 12 inches
1 yellow pepper for garnish (optional)
Fruit-dipping sauce
1 cup pineapple juice
¼ tsp. finely chopped fresh ginger
½ lemon, grated zest and strained juice
1 tsp. low-sodium soy sauce
¼ tsp. tomato paste
1 tsp. cornstarch, dissolved in 1½ tsp. water
2 scallions, finely chopped

In a shallow dish, mix the cornstarch with the sherry or sake, ¼ teaspoon of the salt, and some ground white pepper. Coat the chicken with this mixture and allow it to stand for 10 minutes.

Strain the cloud-ear mushrooms, squeeze them dry, and finely shred them. If you are using fresh shiitake mushrooms, thinly slice them.

Beat the egg until it is frothy. Heat a small, nonstick frying pan over medium heat and pour in the egg to make a thin omelet. Allow the omelet to cool, then cut it into fine shreds.

Place a wok over high heat until it is very hot, add ½ teaspoon of the oil, and stir-fry the chicken for 20 to 30 seconds. Remove the chicken from the wok and keep it warm. Add 1 teaspoon of the oil to the wok, and fry the garlic and ginger for 10 seconds, then add the mushrooms and stir-fry for 20 seconds. Finally, add the bean sprouts, green pepper, and carrot, and stir-fry for 20 seconds more, adding the remaining salt and some pepper halfway through. Remove the wok from the heat. Let it cool, then mix in the shredded omelet and the chicken.

Preheat the oven to 400° F.

Divide the filling mixture into 32 parts. Keeping the sheets of phyllo pastry stacked, cut each into four strips measuring about 4½ by 12 inches. Cover the stacks of

phyllo you are not working on with a damp dishtowel to prevent them from drying out and becoming brittle. Brush one strip of phyllo lightly with oil and place a portion of filling along one of the shorter ends, leaving ½ inch uncovered on either side. Roll the phyllo around the filling a couple of times, fold the uncovered edges in, and continue rolling until you reach the other end. Place the roll seam side down on a lightly oiled or nonstick baking sheet. Repeat with the remaining phyllo strips and filling. Bake the rolls, turning once, until they are golden brown—15 to 20 minutes.

Meanwhile, prepare the sauce. In a nonreactive saucepan, reduce the pineapple juice by half over high heat. Add the ginger and the lemon zest and juice, and cook over medium-low heat for one minute; then add the soy sauce, the tomato paste, and the cornstarch mixture, and heat through. Remove the pan from the heat and add the scallions.

Slice off the top of the yellow pepper, if you are using it, and remove the ribs and seeds to make a container for the dipping sauce; alternatively, spoon the dipping sauce into a bowl. Serve the spring rolls on a warmed serving platter.

EDITOR'S NOTE: *The omelet will absorb any moisture from the vegetables during cooking and ensure that the pastry remains crisp. You can substitute ¼ cup of lightly toasted bread-crumbs, but the egg adds more flavor to the rolls.*

Turkey Twists

Makes 20 twists
Working time: about 30 minutes
Total time: about 3 hours (includes marinating)

Per twist:
Calories **25**
Protein **5g.**
Cholesterol **10mg.**
Total fat **trace**
Saturated fat **trace**
Sodium **50mg.**

10 oz. turkey breast meat	
2 limes, the outer layer of zest removed with a peeler and cut into 20 leaf shapes	
4 oz. cranberries	
2 tsp. honey	
Lime-ginger marinade	
1 tbsp. freshly grated ginger	
1 garlic clove, crushed	
1 tbsp. honey	
1 lime, grated zest and 1 tbsp. juice only	
2 tbsp. plain low-fat yogurt	
½ tsp. salt	
hot red-pepper sauce	

To make the marinade, put the ginger, garlic, honey, lime zest and juice, yogurt, salt, and some hot red-pepper sauce into a bowl, and stir well until evenly blended. Thinly slice the turkey, then cut the slices into strips measuring about 5 by ½ inches. Place the strips in the marinade and turn to coat them evenly. Set aside in a cool place to marinate for two to three hours.

Soak 20 bamboo skewers in water for 10 to 15 minutes to keep them from burning under the broiler.

Place the lime leaves, cranberries, and honey in a small saucepan with about 2 tablespoons of water, and cook over low heat until the cranberries begin to soften—three to four minutes. Drain the cranberries and limes, and set aside. Preheat the broiler.

Thread each turkey strip onto the end of a skewer to form a continuous double *s* shape, skewering a cranberry between each loop of the *s.*

Line a baking sheet with parchment paper. Arrange the turkey twists on the sheet and broil, turning once, until the turkey is tender and the coating begins to color—12 to 15 minutes.

Garnish the end of each skewer with a lime leaf and arrange the twists on a serving plate.

Pork Phyllo Pastries

Makes 12 pastries
Working time: about 20 minutes
Total time: about 1 hour and 10 minutes
(includes marinating)

Per pastry:
Calories **55**
Protein **4g.**
Cholesterol **15mg.**
Total fat **3g.**
Saturated fat **2g.**
Sodium **15mg.**

10 oz. pork loin, trimmed of fat, finely chopped
1 tbsp. dry sherry or rice wine
1 tbsp. low-sodium soy sauce
1 tsp. finely chopped fresh ginger
3 tbsp. chopped scallions
freshly ground black pepper
3 sheets phyllo pastry, each about 18 by 12 inches
2 tbsp. unsalted butter, melted

Place the pork in a shallow, nonreactive bowl with the sherry or rice wine, soy sauce, the chopped ginger and scallions, and some pepper, and allow the mixture to marinate at room temperature for 20 minutes.

Preheat the oven to 400° F.

Cut each phyllo sheet into quarters and fold each quarter in half crosswise. Line 12 cups of a muffin pan with the phyllo, allowing the edges to overhang. Divide the pork mixture among the cups. Brush the overhanging phyllo edges with some of the melted butter, then fold the edges over the mixture to resemble the petals of a flower; twist the edges slightly to keep them in place. Brush the phyllo again with the remaining melted butter, then cover the tray with aluminium foil and cook in the oven for 20 minutes. Remove the foil and bake the pastries about 10 minutes more to allow the phyllo to become golden brown.

Serve the pastries hot.

EDITOR'S NOTE: *These pork pastries may also be served at room temperature.*

Thai-Style Parcels

THE INGREDIENTS FOR THIS DISH ARE PREPARED BY THE
COOK AND PRESENTED AT THE TABLE FOR EACH GUEST TO
ASSEMBLE INDIVIDUALLY.

Makes 48 parcels
Working time: about 1 hour
Total time: about 4 hours (includes chilling and marinating)

Per parcel:
Calories **30**
Protein **3g.**
Cholesterol **10mg.**
Total fat **2g.**
Saturated fat **1g.**
Sodium **25mg.**

12 oz. lean beef tenderloin, trimmed of fat and chilled in the freezer until firm (about 1 hour)
12 oz. boneless chicken breast, skinned
1 Nappa cabbage, washed, dried, and finely shredded
1 large head of lettuce, leaves washed and dried
½ cucumber, peeled in alternate strips with a cannelle knife or peeler, halved lengthwise, and thinly sliced
1 bunch cilantro, leaves only
1 bunch fresh mint, large stalks removed
1 bunch fresh basil, leaves only
48 rice-paper wrappers (about 6 inches in diameter)
1 tbsp. peanut oil
freshly ground black pepper

Spicy marinade

1 oz. tamarind paste, dissolved in ½ cup water for 15 minutes
1 tsp. sambal oelek
1 tbsp. low-sodium soy sauce
1 tsp. anchovy purée
3 garlic cloves, crushed
1½-inch piece fresh ginger, peeled and finely shredded

Lemon glaze

4 tbsp. fresh lemon juice
2 tbsp. low-sodium soy sauce
1 tsp. brown sugar

Dipping sauce

¼ cup fresh lemon juice
4 tbsp. low-sodium soy sauce
2 tsp. sambal oelek
½-inch piece fresh ginger, peeled and finely shredded
1 small stick fresh lemon grass, finely chopped (optional)

To make the marinade, strain the tamarind liquid and discard the solids. Add the sambal oelek, soy sauce, anchovy purée, garlic, and ginger to the liquid, and stir well to blend the ingredients. Divide the marinade between two shallow dishes. Cut the beef into very thin slices across the grain, then cut the slices into strips about ½ inch wide. Cut the chicken breast into thin strips of the same width. Place the beef in one of the marinade dishes and the chicken in the other; stir to coat the strips evenly, and let them marinate in a cool place for three hours.

Shortly before serving, make the glaze by combining the lemon juice, soy sauce, and brown sugar with 2 tablespoons of water in a small saucepan; reduce the glaze to about 3 tablespoons—three to five minutes.

Meanwhile, make the dipping sauce by combining the lemon juice, soy sauce, sambal oelek, ginger, and lemon grass, if you are using it, with 4 tablespoons of water. Pour the sauce into dipping bowls. Arrange the Nappa cabbage, lettuce leaves, and cucumber slices on a serving platter, and the cilantro, mint, and basil on a second platter. Set out the rice-paper wrappers and bowls of tepid water for dipping the wrappers.

In a wok or a wide, heavy-bottomed frying pan, heat the oil until it is sizzling. Remove the strips of beef from the marinade, and sear them for about 20 seconds, stirring and tossing the meat with a spatula. Remove the beef from the wok and keep it warm. Cook the chicken pieces in the wok until the flesh is no longer translucent—about 45 seconds.

Arrange the beef and chicken on separate serving dishes, and brush with the glaze. Serve immediately, with the raw ingredients, pepper, and sauce, for each guest to make into parcels (box, below).

EDITOR'S NOTE: *Less familiar ingredients, described in the glossary on pages 140-141, are available at Oriental groceries.*

Rice-Paper Packages

MAKING A PARCEL. Dip a rice-paper wrapper in a bowl of tepid water, gently shake off any excess water, and place the softened wrapper in the palm of your hand or on a small plate. Place small quantities of ingredients in the center of the wrapper, and fold the edges over the filling to enclose it. Then dip the parcel in the sauce.

Thai Skewers

Makes 18 skewers
Working time: about 25 minutes
Total time: about 2 hours and 40 minutes
(includes chilling)

Per skewer:
Calories **55**
Protein **6g.**
Cholesterol **40mg.**
Total fat **2g.**
Saturated fat **trace**
Sodium **90mg.**

½ lb. pork tenderloin or loin, trimmed of fat
12 oz. large shrimp, peeled and deveined if necessary
3½ oz. crabmeat, picked over
3 garlic cloves
1-inch piece fresh ginger, peeled
½ tsp. fresh lime juice
¼ tsp. grated lime zest
1 tsp. ground lemon grass
3 tbsp. chopped cilantro
1 tbsp. chopped fresh basil
½ tsp. salt
freshly ground black pepper
1 tsp. arrowroot
½ beaten egg white
1 papaya, peeled and cut into ½-inch cubes
1 tbsp. safflower oil
Aromatic dip
2 tbsp. low-sodium soy sauce
1 tbsp. fresh lime juice
1 tbsp. dark brown sugar
1 garlic clove
½-inch piece fresh ginger, peeled
fine strips of fresh chili pepper (cautionary note, page 18)
thinly sliced scallion for garnish (optional)

Finely chop the pork in a food processor, then transfer it to a large bowl. Process the shrimp to a fine paste and add it to the pork, then process and add the crabmeat. Mix the pork and shellfish together well with your hands.

Using a garlic press, squeeze the juice from the garlic and ginger into the pork and shellfish mixture. Add the lime juice and zest, lemon grass, cilantro, basil, salt, and some pepper. Mix the ingredients together. Stir the arrowroot into the egg white until no lumps remain, and blend this mixture into the pork and fish. Chill for at least two hours.

To make the dip, combine the soy sauce and lime juice with 2 tablespoons of water in a small bowl, and dissolve the sugar in the mixture. Using a garlic press, squeeze the juice from the garlic and ginger into the mixture. Add the chili pepper and the scallion, if you are using it, and pour the dip into a serving bowl.

Preheat the broiler. Soak 18 wooden satay sticks or skewers in water for about 10 minutes to prevent them from burning under the broiler.

Form the chilled pork and shellfish mixture into 54 small balls, each about ¾ inch in diameter. Thread three balls onto each skewer, alternating them with cubes of papaya.

Brush a broiler pan lightly with a little of the safflower oil, and arrange the skewers in a single layer in the pan. Brush the balls and the papaya cubes lightly with the remaining oil. Cook the skewers, turning once, until they are golden brown—about 10 minutes. Serve immediately, accompanied by the dip.

Stuffed Pasta Rings

Makes 24 rings
Working time: about 20 minutes
Total time: about 30 minutes

Per ring:
Calories **40**
Protein **2g.**
Cholesterol **trace**
Total fat **1g.**
Saturated fat **trace**
Sodium **70mg.**

4 thin slices whole-wheat bread, crusts removed
3 manicotti tubes (about 2 oz.)
3 oz. low-fat mozzarella, grated (about 6 tbsp.)
3 tbsp. rolled oats
1 oz. very thinly sliced prosciutto for garnish
flat-leaf parsley for garnish
Tomato and basil filling
4 scallions, finely chopped
1 small garlic clove, crushed
2 medium tomatoes, peeled, seeded (technique, page 76), and chopped
2 tsp. tomato paste
1 tsp. finely chopped fresh basil
½ tsp. honey
freshly ground black pepper

To prepare the tomato and basil filling, place the scallions, garlic, tomatoes, and tomato paste in a small saucepan. Cook over medium heat, stirring occasionally, until the mixture is pulpy and thick. Stir in the basil,

honey, and some pepper, remove the pan from the heat, and set aside.

Flatten the slices of bread with a rolling pin, then cut six rounds from each slice using a 1-inch plain cutter. Toast the bread rounds in a hot oven until they are browned. Space them evenly on a baking sheet.

Cook the manicotti in 2 quarts of lightly salted boiling water until it is just tender—8 to 10 minutes. Drain the pasta and rinse it well under cold running water, then thread each pasta tube onto a wooden spoon handle to prevent it from closing up.

Mix the mozzarella and rolled oats together. Using the round cutter, cut out 24 rounds of prosciutto; set aside for a garnish.

Cut each pasta tube into eight rings and place the rings on the toast rounds. Divide the mozzarella and oat mixture in half; distribute one portion among the pasta rings, a little into each ring. Divide the tomato filling equally among the pasta rings, then sprinkle with the remaining mozzarella mixture. Place the baking sheet under a hot broiler and broil until the topping begins to brown—three to four minutes.

Garnish each canapé with a folded piece of prosciutto and a parsley leaf. Serve warm.

EDITOR'S NOTE: *These canapés may also be served at room temperature.*

Veal with Apricot and Nut Stuffing

Makes 32 slices
Working time: about 15 minutes
Total time: about 1 hour and 25 minutes
(includes soaking)

Per slice:
Calories **45**
Protein **5g.**
Cholesterol **15mg.**
Total fat **2g.**
Saturated fat **1g.**
Sodium **40mg.**

4 veal cutlets (about 6 oz. each), pounded thin
1 tsp. safflower oil
cilantro or parsley sprigs for garnish
Apricot and nut stuffing
4 oz. dried apricots, covered with boiling water and soaked for at least 1 hour, chopped
1 tbsp. finely chopped scallion
2 oz. unsalted cashew nuts, finely chopped
2 tsp. chopped cilantro or fresh parsley
6 cardamom pods, crushed seeds only
4 tbsp. fresh orange juice
¼ tsp. salt
freshly ground black pepper

Preheat the oven to 400° F. Line a baking sheet with parchment paper.

To make the stuffing, place the apricots, scallion, cashew nuts, cilantro or parsley, cardamom seeds, orange juice, salt, and some freshly ground black pepper in a heavy-bottomed saucepan. Cook over medium heat, stirring occasionally, until the mixture softens—about two minutes.

Cut the veal cutlets in half across their width. Divide the stuffing among the pieces of veal, spreading it evenly to the edges. Neatly roll up each piece, and secure it with two cocktail sticks or small skewers. Place the rolls on the baking sheet and brush the meat lightly with the oil.

Bake the rolls in the center of the oven until the veal is lightly browned—five to eight minutes. Allow the rolls to cool for a few minutes, then remove the cocktail sticks and cut each roll into four slices.

Serve immediately, garnished with the cilantro or the sprigs of parsley.

EDITOR'S NOTE: *The apricots may be replaced with soaked dried peaches, apples, or prunes, or a mixture of dried fruit. This snack may also be served at room temperature.*

Spiced Steak Phyllo Boats

Makes 30 boats
Working (and total) time: about 50 minutes

6 sheets phyllo pastry, each about 18 by 12 inches
1½ tbsp. virgin olive oil
1 small onion, very finely chopped
¼ cup pine nuts
2 garlic cloves, crushed
1 tsp. ground cumin
1 tsp. ground cardamom
⅛ tsp. cayenne pepper
¼ tsp. ground cinnamon
¼ lb. mushrooms, finely chopped
⅓ cup raisins, chopped
½ lb. rump steak, trimmed of fat, finely chopped
¼ tsp. salt
freshly ground black pepper
1 tbsp. finely cut chives

Preheat the oven to 425° F. Lay out three sheets of phyllo pastry, one on top of another, on a work surface. Using an inverted 4½-by-2-inch boat-shaped tartlet mold as a guide, cut out oval shapes from the pastry. Fit the ovals into 3½-by-1½-inch boat-shaped molds, pressing the pastry firmly into position. Trim the pointed ends into shape with scissors. Repeat with the remaining pastry until you have filled 30 tartlet molds. Place the molds on baking sheets and bake in the oven until the pastry is golden brown—six to eight minutes. Carefully remove the phyllo boats from the molds and set them on wire racks to cool.

To make the filling, heat half of the oil in a frying pan. Add the onion, and cook over medium-low heat until it is soft but not browned—five to six minutes. Add the pine nuts, garlic, cumin, cardamom, cayenne pepper, and cinnamon. Cook for two to three minutes, then add the mushrooms, and cook until they are soft and most of the liquid has evaporated—six to eight minutes. Stir in the raisins. Transfer the mushroom mixture from the pan to a plate, and set it aside.

Heat the remaining oil in the frying pan until it is hot but not smoking. Add the steak and stir-fry it just long enough for the meat to change color—do not overcook. Return the mushroom mixture to the pan and heat through. Season with the salt and some pepper.

Spoon the filling into the phyllo boats and sprinkle with the chives. Serve warm.

EDITOR'S NOTE: *The phyllo cases may be prepared ahead of time and stored in an airtight container.*

Making Sausages

1 *PREPARING THE CASING. Roll a length of casing onto the nozzle of a meat grinder, as here, or a funnel or pastry bag, leaving 2 inches hanging. Fill the bowl with the stuffing and turn the handle. When the stuffing just emerges from the nozzle, tie a knot in the casing.*

2 *FILLING THE CASING. Continue turning the handle to fill the casing; use a wooden spoon to push the meat down. As the stuffing is fed into the casing, gradually slip the casing off the nozzle; use your fingers to prevent overstretching and to eliminate any air bubbles.*

3 *FORMING LINKS. When only about 2 inches of the casing remains to be filled, slip it off the nozzle and knot it. Roll the casing on a work surface to even out the stuffing. To form links, twist the lengths through three or four turns at intervals of about 1 inch.*

Little Beef Sausages with Horseradish

Makes about 60 sausages
Working time: about 35 minutes
Total time: about 1 hour and 45 minutes
(includes soaking)

Per sausage:	⅔ *cup fresh breadcrumbs*
Calories **25**	*2 shallots, finely chopped*
Protein **3g.**	*1 garlic clove, crushed*
Cholesterol **5mg.**	*1 tbsp. chopped parsley*
Total fat **1g.**	*2 tsp. chopped fresh thyme*
Saturated fat **trace**	*1 tsp. chopped fresh sage*
Sodium **35mg.**	

1 lb. ground or very finely chopped lean beef
¼ *cup rolled oats*
2 tsp. Dijon mustard
½ *tsp. salt*
freshly ground black pepper
2 egg whites
6 feet natural lamb sausage casing, soaked in acidulated water for 1 hour
1 tsp. safflower oil
Horseradish dip
1 tbsp. red wine vinegar
1 tsp. Dijon mustard
1 tsp. fresh lemon juice
¼ *tsp. salt*
freshly ground black pepper
½ *cup plain low-fat yogurt*
1½ *tbsp. grated horseradish*
lemon slice for garnish (optional)

Preheat the oven to 400° F. Brush a nonstick dish or baking pan lightly with oil.

In a large bowl, combine the breadcrumbs, shallots, garlic, parsley, thyme, and sage. Add the beef and mix well. Add the rolled oats, mustard, salt, some freshly ground black pepper, and the egg whites, and mix together all the ingredients.

Unravel the sausage casing and cut it in half. Carefully roll one end of a length of casing over the spout of a funnel, and run cold water through it to open it out, then rinse the other length in the same way. Drain the sausage casings. Make up the 1-inch sausages as shown above.

Place the linked sausages in the dish or baking pan, and brush them lightly with the safflower oil. Bake in the oven until they are golden brown—10 to 15 minutes. While the sausages are cooking, mix together the vinegar, mustard, lemon juice, salt, some pepper, the yogurt, and horseradish to make the dip. Put the dip into a bowl, garnished with the lemon, if you wish.

Cut through the links with kitchen scissors or a small, sharp knife, and place the sausages on a serving plate. Serve immediately with the horseradish dip.

EDITOR'S NOTE: *Natural sausage casings—the cleansed intestines of lamb, pig, or cow—can be ordered from your butcher or from specialty suppliers. Lamb casings are usually used for small sausages. Lean pork, veal, lamb, or a mixture of meats may be substituted for the beef.*

Sausage Rolls

Makes 40 rolls
Working time: about 1 hour
Total time: about 1 hour and 25 minutes

Per roll:
Calories **50**
Protein **2g.**
Cholesterol **5mg.**
Total fat **3g.**
Saturated fat **1g.**
Sodium **80mg.**

20 thin slices whole-wheat bread
2 tbsp. Dijon mustard
4 tbsp. polyunsaturated margarine
2 tsp. tomato paste
2 garlic cloves, crushed
Pork sausage meat
14 oz. pork shoulder, trimmed of excess fat
1 onion, chopped
6 tbsp. fresh whole-wheat breadcrumbs
2 tbsp. polyunsaturated margarine
¼ tsp. salt
freshly ground black pepper
2 tsp. mixed dried herbs

To make the sausage meat, cut the pork into strips, and pass the meat and onion through the fine blade of a meat grinder into a bowl, or finely chop the meat in a food processor. Mix in the breadcrumbs, margarine, salt, some freshly ground black pepper, and the herbs, then pass the mixture through the grinder once again, or blend it in the processor.

Preheat the oven to 425° F.

Grease several baking sheets.

Remove the crusts from the bread, then roll each slice with a rolling pin to make it pliable. Set aside.

Divide the sausage-meat mixture into five equal portions, then shape each portion into a sausage shape about 16 inches long. Cut each sausage into four 4-inch-long pieces.

Spread each slice of bread with the mustard. Put a length of sausage meat on one edge of each slice. Roll the bread up to enclose the sausage meat, ending with the seam underneath.

Put the margarine, tomato paste, and garlic into a small bowl, and beat well together until the mixture is very soft. Brush the garlic mixture evenly over the sausage rolls. Cut each roll in half. Place the sausage rolls, seam side down, on the prepared baking sheets, and cook in the oven until they are golden brown and crisp—about 25 minutes. Serve warm.

Ham and Date Pinwheels

Makes 40 pinwheels
Working time: about 15 minutes
Total time: about 20 minutes

Per pinwheel:
Calories **40**
Protein **2g.**
Cholesterol **5mg.**
Total fat **2g.**
Saturated fat **1g.**
Sodium **125mg.**

10 large, thin slices whole-wheat sandwich bread, crusts removed
10 fresh or dried dates, halved and pitted
20 thin slices lean ham, 2 by 4 inches
1 tsp. honey
parsley sprigs for garnish
Tomato filling
2 medium tomatoes, peeled, seeded (technique, page 76), and chopped
1 tsp. tomato paste
1 shallot, finely chopped
1 bay leaf
freshly ground black pepper

To prepare the tomato filling, put the tomatoes, tomato paste, shallot, bay leaf, and some freshly ground black pepper into a small, heavy-bottomed saucepan. Cook over medium heat, stirring occasionally, until the mixture has thickened. Remove the pan from the heat and set aside.

Preheat the oven to 400° F.

Flatten each slice of bread with a rolling pin, and trim it into a neat rectangle with its shorter sides the length of two dates laid end to end.

Take one piece of bread and spread it sparingly with some of the tomato filling. Lay two date halves end to end along a short edge of the slice, and roll up the bread firmly. Cut the bread roll in half between the two dates. Wrap a piece of ham around one of the rolls, ensuring that the ham covers the seam of the bread, and secure with two wooden cocktail sticks. Cut the roll in half between the cocktail sticks to make two pinwheels. Wrap and cut the other roll.

Repeat this process with the remaining bread, dates, and ham to make 40 pinwheels. Place the pinwheels on a baking sheet lined with parchment paper. Warm the honey in a small pan and brush each roll lightly with it, then bake the pinwheels in the oven until the ham is cooked—five to eight minutes.

Arrange the pinwheels on a serving plate and garnish with the parsley sprigs.

EDITOR'S NOTE: *You can vary this recipe by using soaked prunes or fresh apricots instead of dates.*

Beef-Heart Brochettes

Makes 16 brochettes
Working time: about 15 minutes
Total time: about 1 day (includes marinating)

Per brochette:
Calories **50**
Protein **8g.**
Cholesterol **35mg.**
Total fat **2g.**
Saturated fat **1g.**
Sodium **95mg.**

1 lb. beef heart, trimmed of fat
5 garlic cloves, crushed
3 fresh red or green chili peppers (cautionary note, page 18), seeded, finely chopped
2 tsp. cayenne pepper
2 tsp. safflower oil
3 tbsp. red wine vinegar
½ tsp. salt
freshly ground black pepper

Cut the heart into 1-inch cubes—you should have about 48 cubes. Mix the garlic, chilies, cayenne pep-per, oil, vinegar, salt, and some pepper together in a large dish. Add the beef-heart cubes and turn to coat them well. Cover the dish and let the beef marinate in the refrigerator for about 24 hours.

Ten minutes before broiling the beef heart, soak 16 wooden skewers about 8 inches long in water to prevent them from scorching under the broiler. Preheat the broiler. Thread the cubes of beef heart onto the skewers, reserving any marinade left in the dish, and cook the brochettes for two to three minutes on one side. Turn, brush with the reserved marinade, and cook for two minutes more. The meat should be well browned on all sides.

EDITOR'S NOTE: *Cubes of lean beef steak may be substituted for the beef heart.*

3 *Tomatoes, prosciutto, and low-fat mozzarella fill the baked dough squares known as calzone (recipe, page 123).*

Sandwiches and Hearty Snacks

According to legend, in 1792, the Earl of Sandwich, too engrossed at the card table to stop for dinner, called for meat served between two slices of bread, and thus gave his name to an entire culinary genre. While retaining the essence of the earl's original concept, the sandwiches presented in this chapter offer multiple variations on his theme to suit endless occasions. Wrought into pinwheels with mushrooms or watercress *(page 106),* they make a filling diversion for a grand reception; thin and crustless, with a cucumber filling *(page 104),* they grace the traditional English tea table; and as chunky baguettes filled with hot shrimp and garlic *(page 114),* sandwiches provide a satisfying midnight meal.

Some sandwiches that follow do away with the top layer of bread. For a sustaining hot snack, a slice of toast can be topped simply with a savory mushroom mixture *(page 118)* or, Catalan style, with tomatoes and ham *(page 112).* For a buffet lunch or dinner, Danish-style open sandwiches *(pages 110-111)* offer another highly decorative variation.

Whatever the context, the key to a successful sandwich is the bread used to make it. Homemade bread is hard to surpass *(page 10),* but more convenient is the wide variety of commercial breads available: wholewheat loaves; rye bread flecked with caraway or cumin seeds; and crusty rolls and baguettes. Mexican tortillas and Italian pizza crusts make novel variations, while the popular Middle Eastern pita, warmed through and slit open, makes a capacious pouch that is virtually all crust and very little crumb.

While unnecessary fat has been kept to a minimum in these recipes, bear in mind that butter or margarine is an integral part of most cold sandwiches, acting as a protective barrier between the bread and the filling. To maximize its benefit while minimizing your intake, spread it in a very thin, even layer. In the occasional exception, such as the Provençale sandwich on page 113, butter is omitted so that the juice-soaked bread becomes as much a feature as the filling.

Most of the sandwiches can be prepared in advance, provided they are tightly covered with plastic wrap to prevent them from drying out. Open sandwiches, however, should be assembled just before serving so as to maximize the appeal of their fresh appearance. And while pizza dough can be left to rise in the refrigerator for up to 24 hours, the pizzas themselves are at their best straight from the oven.

In addition to bread-based snacks, this chapter offers a few other substantial dishes—such as baked oysters *(page 120)*—that are ideal as a sustaining snack for family or friends.

Cucumber Sandwiches

Makes 48 sandwiches
Working time: about 30 minutes
Total time: about 50 minutes (includes chilling)

Per sandwich:	1 cucumber
Calories **25**	¼ tsp. salt
Protein **trace**	4 tbsp. unsalted butter, softened
Cholesterol **5mg.**	2 tbsp. chopped fresh dill, or 1½ tsp. dried dill
Total fat **1g.**	freshly ground black pepper
Saturated fat **trace**	12 thin slices white bread
Sodium **35mg.**	

Using a vegetable peeler, remove the skin from the cucumber. Cut the cucumber into very thin slices. Put the slices into a large bowl and sprinkle them with the salt. Cover the bowl and refrigerate the cucumber slices for at least 30 minutes—during this time, the salt will draw out excess moisture from the cucumber and make it crisp.

Meanwhile, put the butter into a bowl with the dill and some black pepper. Beat well together. Arrange the slices of bread on a work surface, in matching pairs, and spread each one with the dill butter.

Drain the cucumber slices in a colander, then pat them dry on paper towels. Arrange the cucumber slices neatly on six of the bread slices, then sandwich together with the remaining slices. Press the sandwiches firmly together. Carefully remove the crusts and cut each sandwich into four squares, then cut each square in half diagonally to make two triangles. Arrange the sandwiches on a serving plate.

Salmon and Watercress Rolls

Makes 36 rolls
Working time: about 40 minutes
Total time: about 2 hours and 50 minutes (includes cooling and chilling)

Per roll:
Calories **50**
Protein **5g.**
Cholesterol **15mg.**
Total fat **3g.**
Saturated fat **1g.**
Sodium **60mg.**

12 oz. salmon steaks
1 bay leaf
1 sprig thyme
1 sprig parsley
1 slice lemon
8 black peppercorns
¼ tsp. salt
2 tbsp. sour cream
1 tsp. Dijon mustard
freshly ground black pepper
12 thin slices whole-wheat sandwich bread
½ bunch watercress (4 oz.) stemmed, washed, and dried
4 tbsp. unsalted butter, softened

Rinse the salmon steaks under cold running water. Place them in a shallow saucepan with the bay leaf, thyme, parsley, lemon, peppercorns, half of the salt, and 2 tablespoons of water. Cover the pan with a tight-fitting lid and simmer gently over medium heat until the salmon flakes easily—8 to 10 minutes. Remove the saucepan from the heat and allow the salmon to cool in the liquid for about one hour.

When the salmon has cooled, carefully remove the skin and bones. Flake the flesh and put it into a bowl. Add the sour cream, mustard, the remaining salt, and some pepper, and mix gently together.

Remove the crusts from the bread. Roll each slice with a rolling pin to compress the bread slightly and make it pliable.

Finely chop the watercress, then put it into a bowl with the butter and beat well. Spread each slice of bread with the watercress butter. Divide the salmon mixture equally among the slices of bread, then spread it evenly over each slice. Neatly roll up the slices of bread, like jelly rolls, to enclose the salmon. Wrap each roll individually in plastic wrap to prevent drying, and refrigerate for about one hour. Just before serving, remove the wrap and cut each salmon roll into thirds.

Party Pinwheels

Makes 240 pinwheels
Working time: about 1 hour and 40 minutes
Total time: about 4 hours (includes chilling)

Per shrimp pinwheel:
Calories **50**
Protein **4g.**
Cholesterol **25mg.**
Total fat **1g.**
Saturated fat **trace**
Sodium **115mg.**

Per watercress pinwheel:
Calories **65**
Protein **3g.**
Cholesterol **trace**
Total fat **4g.**
Saturated fat **1g.**
Sodium **155mg.**

Per mushroom pinwheel:
Calories **60**
Protein **2g.**
Cholesterol **trace**
Total fat **3g.**
Saturated fat **1g.**
Sodium **75mg.**

8 slices day-old white sandwich bread
8 slices day-old whole-wheat sandwich bread
8 slices day-old pumpernickel bread
Shrimp filling
12 oz. cooked, peeled large shrimp
1 tbsp. prepared horseradish
ground white pepper
1 tbsp. tomato paste
1 tsp. grated lemon zest
2 tbsp. sour cream
Watercress filling
2 bunches watercress, washed, thick stems trimmed
¾ cup low-fat ricotta cheese
¼ tsp. grated nutmeg
¼ tsp. salt
Mushroom filling
12 oz. mushrooms, wiped clean and finely chopped
1 tbsp. Madeira or cognac
1 tbsp. Dijon mustard
¼ tsp. salt
½ cup low-fat ricotta cheese
½ tsp. ground coriander

To make the shrimp filling, blend together the shrimp, horseradish, some white pepper, the tomato paste, lemon zest, and sour cream in a food processor to produce a dense but very smooth purée. Put the purée into the refrigerator to chill.

To make the watercress filling, plunge the water-cress into lightly boiling water for a few seconds, until it is bright green in color and slightly limp. Rinse immediately under cold running water, drain, and squeeze hard. In a food processor, blend the water-cress with the ricotta cheese, nutmeg, and salt to form a speckled green purée. Put the purée into the refrigerator to chill.

To make the mushroom filling, put the mushrooms into a sauté pan with the Madeira or cognac, the mustard, and salt. Cover the pan and cook over low heat until the mushrooms are cooked through—about 10 minutes. Remove the lid and continue to cook to evaporate any excess liquid, then cool the mushroom mixture. Place the cooked mushrooms in a food processor with the ricotta cheese and coriander, and process to form a smooth, light brown purée. Chill the purée for about 30 minutes.

Meanwhile, trim the crusts off the bread and flatten each slice with a rolling pin to make it more flexible. Cover the bread with plastic wrap or a clean, damp cloth until you are ready to use it.

Spread one-eighth of the shrimp mixture on each slice of white bread, one-eighth of the watercress purée on each slice of whole-wheat bread, and one-eighth of the mushroom mixture on each slice of pumpernickel bread. Make sure that the filling extends to the edges of the bread. Roll up each slice, starting with a shorter side, to make a tight roll, but take care not to press out any filling. Wrap the rolls in plastic wrap and chill them for about two hours in the refrigerator.

Unwrap the rolls and use a sharp, serrated knife to slice each one into 10 to 12 thin slices; you may need to discard the first and last slices if they are ragged. Arrange the pinwheels decoratively on a plate to serve.

Seafood Sandwich Gâteau

Serves 12
Working time: about 2 hours
Total time: about 4 hours (includes chilling)

Calories **275**
Protein **17g.**
Cholesterol **50mg.**
Total fat **14g.**
Saturated fat **3g.**
Sodium **485mg.**

10 oz. salmon fillet
1 bay leaf
1 sprig parsley, plus 8 tbsp. chopped parsley
½ small onion
8 black peppercorns
12 oz. Dover or lemon sole or flounder fillets, skinned
1¼ cups unsalted fish stock (recipe, page 139)
1 tbsp. unsalted butter
2 tbsp. unbleached all-purpose flour
3 tbsp. sour cream
1 tbsp. chopped fresh dill
½ tsp. salt
freshly ground black pepper
6 oz. crabmeat, picked over
1 large loaf day-old unsliced whole-wheat sandwich bread
6 tbsp. polyunsaturated margarine
6 lettuce leaves, washed, dried, and shredded
8 radicchio leaves, washed, dried, and shredded
Ricotta-cheese coating
6 tbsp. low-fat ricotta cheese
3 tbsp. sour cream
1 garlic clove, crushed

Remove all the bones from the salmon and trim any membrane. Put the salmon into a saucepan, cover with cold water, and add the bay leaf, parsley sprig, onion, and peppercorns. Cover the pan and bring to a boil. Lower the heat and simmer for five minutes. Remove from the heat and let the salmon cool in the water.

Put the sole or flounder fillets into a shallow saucepan and cover with the fish stock. Cook over medium-low heat until the flesh flakes easily—five to six minutes. Transfer the fillets to a plate and flake the flesh. Strain the fish stock and then boil it until it is reduced to ½ cup. Melt the butter and stir in the flour. Gradually stir in the reduced stock. Bring to a boil, stirring all the time, then lower the heat and simmer gently for two to three minutes, stirring frequently. Remove the pan from the heat. Stir the flaked sole and 2 tablespoons of the chopped parsley into the sauce. Pour the mixture into a bowl, and cover the surface closely with plastic wrap to prevent a skin from forming. Let the mixture cool, then refrigerate until it is chilled.

Flake the salmon and put it into a bowl. Add 2 tablespoons of the sour cream, the dill, a little of the salt, and some pepper. Mix gently, cover, and set aside.

Put the crabmeat into a bowl with the remaining sour cream and salt, and some pepper. Mix together, cover, and set aside.

Cut the bottom crust from the bread. Slicing horizontally, cut six ¼-inch-thick slices from the loaf. Re- ▶

move the crusts, then stack and trim the slices to form a neat oblong about 8 by 4 inches.

Lift the top five slices of bread together; invert the pile and place it next to the bottom slice.

Spread the bottom slice of bread with a thin layer of margarine, then spread the crab mixture evenly on top. Spread the slice of bread on top of the pile with a thin layer of margarine, then place it margarine side down on the crabmeat. Spread the top side with margarine.

Arrange shredded lettuce over this next slice. Spread the next slice on the pile with margarine and place it margarine side down on the lettuce. Spread with margarine and then with the salmon mixture.

Spread the next slice on the pile with a very thin layer of margarine and place it margarine side down on the salmon mixture. Spread with a thin layer of margarine

and cover with an even layer of shredded radicchio.

Spread the next slice of bread with margarine and place it margarine side down on the radicchio. Spread with margarine, then with the sole mixture. Spread the remaining slice of bread with margarine and place it margarine side down on the sole.

Press the layers firmly together, then wrap tightly in plastic wrap. Refrigerate for one hour.

To make the coating, beat the ricotta cheese with the sour cream and garlic until the mixture is smooth and creamy. Unwrap the chilled loaf and place it on a flat serving board. Spread the ricotta-cheese mixture evenly over the loaf, coating it completely.

Sprinkle the loaf liberally with the remaining chopped parsley, pressing it gently into the cheese coating. Refrigerate for about one hour before serving.

Chicken and Asparagus Sandwich Gâteau

Serves 12
Working time: about 1 hour and 30 minutes
Total time: about 4 hours and 45 minutes (includes chilling)

Calories **180**
Protein **10g.**
Cholesterol **30mg.**
Total fat **9g.**
Saturated fat **3g.**
Sodium **250mg.**

12 oz. skinned and boned chicken breasts
1¼ cups unsalted chicken stock (recipe, page 139)
4 tbsp. unsalted butter, softened
2 tbsp. unbleached all-purpose flour
½ lb. asparagus, trimmed and peeled
2 tbsp. polyunsaturated margarine
2 tbsp. chopped fresh marjoram, or 2 tsp. dried marjoram
¼ tsp. salt
freshly ground black pepper
1 large loaf day-old unsliced white sandwich bread
½ small head lettuce, leaves washed, dried, and shredded
1 tbsp. finely shredded basil leaves
1 tsp. paprika
Ricotta-cheese coating
6 tbsp. low-fat ricotta cheese
2½ tbsp. sour cream
1 garlic clove, crushed
2 tsp. mixed fresh chopped herbs, or 1 tsp. mixed dried herbs

Put the chicken into a pan with the stock, cover, and cook over medium-low heat until the meat is tender— 10 to 15 minutes. Let the chicken cool in the stock.

Remove the chicken from the stock and finely chop it. Bring the stock to a boil, and boil gently until it is reduced to ½ cup. Blend 1 tablespoon of the butter with the flour in a small bowl, then gradually whisk the mixture into the hot stock. Bring to a boil, stirring until thickened. Lower the heat and simmer for two to three minutes. Stir the chopped chicken into the sauce. Pour the sauce into a bowl and cover the surface closely with plastic wrap to prevent a skin from forming. Let

the sauce cool a little, then refrigerate until it is completely cold—about one hour.

Meanwhile, cook the asparagus in boiling water until it is tender—three to four minutes. Drain the asparagus in a colander and refresh it under cold running water. Drain well.

Combine the remaining butter with the margarine, marjoram, salt, and some pepper. Beat well.

Remove the bottom crust from the loaf of bread. Cut the loaf horizontally into five slices; stack the slices together and remove the crusts to form a neat oblong about 8 by 4 inches. Lift off the top four slices together, and place them upside down next to the bottom slice.

Spread the bottom slice of bread with a thin layer of the marjoram butter, then spread with half of the cold chicken mixture. Spread the slice of bread on top of the pile with butter, and place it buttered side down on top of the chicken mixture. Butter again, then arrange the asparagus stalks neatly on top. (If the stalks are large, slice them in half lengthwise.)

Butter the next slice of bread and place it buttered side down on top of the asparagus. Butter again, then cover with the lettuce and basil.

Butter the next slice of bread and place it buttered side down on top of the lettuce. Spread with butter and then with the remaining chicken mixture.

Spread the remaining slice with butter and place it buttered side down on top of the chicken mixture.

Press the layers firmly together, then wrap tightly in plastic wrap. Refrigerate for one hour.

To make the coating, put the ricotta cheese, sour cream, garlic, and herbs into a bowl, and beat well together. Unwrap the chilled loaf and place it on a flat serving board. Spread the cheese mixture evenly and smoothly over the loaf to coat it completely.

Cut strips of wax paper about ½ inch wide and place them diagonally across the top of the loaf. Sprinkle the loaf liberally with paprika, then remove the wax-paper strips to create alternating bands of red and white. Refrigerate the loaf for one hour before slicing.

Lobster and Crabmeat on Whole-Wheat Bread

Serves 4
Working (and total) time: about 10 minutes

Calories **160**
Protein **10g.**
Cholesterol **50mg.**
Total fat **8g.**
Saturated fat **3g.**
Sodium **320mg.**

1 tbsp. unsalted butter, softened
4 slices whole-wheat sandwich bread
1½ oz. lamb's lettuce, or ½ bunch watercress, stemmed, washed, and dried
3 oz. crabmeat, picked over and flaked
2 cooked lobster tails, shelled and thickly sliced
Sour-cream dressing
3 tbsp. sour cream
1 tsp. fresh lemon juice
¼ tsp. tomato paste
freshly ground black pepper

To make the dressing, put the sour cream, lemon juice, tomato paste, and some pepper into a small bowl. Mix the ingredients together and set aside.

Spread the butter evenly on the bread, and cover with the lamb's lettuce or watercress. Pile the crabmeat on top of the lettuce and add the lobster slices.

Spoon the sour-cream dressing onto the sandwiches before serving.

Salmon and Avocado on Whole-Grain Bread

Serves 4
Working time: about 25 minutes
Total time: about 40 minutes

Calories **215**
Protein **16g.**
Cholesterol **60mg.**
Total fat **12g.**
Saturated fat **4g.**
Sodium **300mg.**

½ lb. salmon or trout fillets
2 tsp. fresh lemon juice
freshly ground black pepper
1 tbsp. unsalted butter, softened
4 slices whole-grain bread
1 tbsp. prepared horseradish
8 curly endive leaves, washed and dried
2-inch piece cucumber, very thinly sliced
1 small avocado
1 tbsp. plain low-fat yogurt (optional)

Preheat the oven to 375° F. Place the salmon or trout fillets on a piece of aluminum foil, and sprinkle them with half the lemon juice and some black pepper. Wrap the fish up tightly in the foil to form a parcel, and bake until the flesh is just firm and cooked through—12 to 15 minutes. Open the parcel and allow the fish to cool slightly, then peel away the skin and discard it.

Butter the bread evenly, then spread each slice with the horseradish. Place two endive leaves on each slice of bread and arrange the cucumber slices on top. Peel and slice the avocado, and arrange the slices on top of the cucumber. Break the fish into small pieces, removing any bones, and divide it among the sandwiches.

To serve, sprinkle the sandwiches with some freshly ground black pepper and the remaining lemon juice. Alternatively, mix the lemon juice with the yogurt and drizzle it over the sandwiches.

Chicken and Fig on Whole-Wheat Bread

Serves 4
Working (and total) time: about 10 minutes

Calories **130**
Protein **13g.**
Cholesterol **40mg.**
Total fat **5g.**
Saturated fat **2g.**
Sodium **120mg.**

1 tbsp. unsalted butter, softened
4 slices whole-wheat bread
2 tsp. cranberry sauce
8 red oakleaf lettuce leaves or other tender lettuce, such as bib or Boston, washed and dried
6 oz. cooked chicken breast, thinly sliced
2 fresh figs, sliced

Butter the bread evenly, then spread each slice with ½ teaspoon of the cranberry sauce.

Place two leaves of lettuce on each piece of bread, and arrange the chicken breast and fig slices on top.

Roast Beef and Radicchio on Rye Bread

Serves 4
Working (and total) time: about 25 minutes

Calories **195**
Protein **13g.**
Cholesterol **40mg.**
Total fat **10g.**
Saturated fat **4g.**
Sodium **60mg.**

4 medium new potatoes (about 6 oz.)
1 tbsp. unsalted butter, softened
4 thin slices dark rye bread
12 radicchio leaves, washed and dried
6 oz. rare roast beef, trimmed of fat and thinly sliced

Mustard dressing
2 tsp. walnut oil
1 tsp. red wine vinegar
⅛ tsp. sugar
1 tsp. grainy mustard
freshly ground black pepper

Scrub the potatoes, and cook them in boiling water until they are cooked but still show resistance when pierced with the tip of a knife—about 10 minutes. Drain them well and let them cool.

While the potatoes are cooking, mix the oil, vinegar, sugar, mustard, and some freshly ground pepper together in a small bowl, and set aside. Spread a thin layer of the butter on the bread and arrange three radicchio leaves on each slice.

Slice the potatoes and divide them among the open sandwiches. Fold the slices of beef and arrange them on top of the potatoes. Spoon a little dressing over each open sandwich and serve.

Tomato and Prosciutto Toasts

Serves 8
Working (and total) time: 20 minutes

Calories **270**
Protein **11g.**
Cholesterol **5mg.**
Total fat **7g.**
Saturated fat **1g.**
Sodium **200mg.**

4 long, crusty rolls	3½ oz. thinly sliced proscuitto, trimmed of fat
2 tomatoes, peeled, seeded (technique, page 76), and finely chopped	
2 garlic cloves, crushed	
2 tbsp. virgin olive oil	
1 tsp. chopped fresh marjoram	
¼ tsp. salt	
freshly ground black pepper	

Cut the rolls in half and toast them on the cut side.

Mix together the tomatoes, garlic, oil, marjoram, salt, and some pepper. Divide the mixture among the rolls, spread it evenly, and press well into the surface. Cut the prosciutto into strips and arrange a few strips over the top of each roll. Serve immediately.

Provençale Sandwich

Serves 4
Working time: about 10 minutes
Total time: about 30 minutes

Per piece:
Calories **305**
Protein **10g.**
Cholesterol **0mg.**
Total fat **15g.**
Saturated fat **2g.**
Sodium **595mg.**

4 tomatoes
2 garlic cloves, crushed
3 tbsp. virgin olive oil
freshly ground black pepper
1 baguette (about 2 feet long), or 4 large, crusty rolls
1 small onion, thinly sliced
1 green pepper, cut into rings
4 canned anchovies, soaked in milk for 20 minutes, drained, rinsed, and patted dry
4 lettuce leaves

Peel *(technique, page 76)* and finely chop one of the tomatoes. Mix the chopped tomato with the garlic, oil, and some pepper.

Split the baguette along one side, without cutting through the crust. Open it out so that it lies flat, and spread the tomato mixture evenly over the bread.

Slice the remaining tomatoes, and place them on one half of the baguette along with the onion and pepper rings. Arrange the anchovies and lettuce leaves on top, and cover with the other half of the baguette.

Press down with your hands to compress the sandwich and allow the flavors to blend. Cut the baguette diagonally into four pieces and serve.

Baguette with Shrimp and Garlic Filling

Serves 6
Working time: about 10 minutes
Total time: about 20 minutes

Calories **165**
Protein **10g.**
Cholesterol **40mg.**
Total fat **5g.**
Saturated fat **trace**
Sodium **340mg.**

¼ cup low-fat ricotta cheese
½ garlic clove, crushed
2 tsp. finely chopped fresh herbs, such as parsley, chives, and dill
1 tsp. fresh lemon juice
freshly ground black pepper
6 oz. cooked medium shrimp, peeled, deveined if necessary, and chopped
1 baguette, about 2 feet long, or 6 large, crusty rolls

Preheat the oven to 425° F. In a medium-size bowl, mix together the ricotta cheese, garlic, herbs, lemon juice, and a few generous grindings of black pepper. Stir in the chopped shrimp.

Cut deep diagonal slashes at 1½-inch intervals in the baguette, taking care not to slice all the way through. Stuff the shrimp mixture into the slashes.

Wrap the baguette or rolls loosely in aluminum foil, and bake in the oven for 10 minutes. Serve hot.

Savory Filled Loaf

Serves 6
Working time: about 25 minutes
Total time: about 1 hour

Calories **80**
Protein **4g.**
Cholesterol **5mg.**
Total fat **3g.**
Saturated fat **1g.**
Sodium **350mg.**

6 oz. mushrooms, wiped clean, and quartered or halved
1 tbsp. safflower oil
1½ tbsp. fresh lemon juice
2 tsp. fresh thyme, or ½ tsp. dried thyme leaves
½ tsp. salt
freshly ground black pepper
1 small, round peasant loaf, about 6 inches in diameter
2 oz. thinly sliced prosciutto
3 tomatoes, peeled, seeded (technique, page 76), and thinly sliced

In a small frying pan, sauté the mushrooms in the oil and lemon juice until their juices run. Stir in the thyme, salt, and some pepper, then set aside.

Preheat the oven to 375° F.

Slice off the top of the loaf to form a lid about 1 inch thick at its center. With your fingers, scoop out bread from the center of the loaf, leaving a ½-inch-thick base and sides; use the scooped-out bread to make bread-crumbs for another dish.

Arrange the mushrooms in the bottom of the bread case. Lay the slices of prosciutto on top of the mush-rooms; the ends of the slices should overhang the sides of the loaf. Arrange the tomatoes on top of the ham, add some pepper, then fold the overhanging ham to enclose the tomatoes. Replace the lid of the loaf.

Wrap the loaf in foil and bake in the oven for 30 minutes. Unwrap the loaf and cut it into wedges.

Serve warm.

Beef-Salad Tortilla Cones

Makes 8 cones
Working time: about 45 minutes
Total time: about 1 hour and 10 minutes

Per cone:
Calories **280**
Protein **9g.**
Cholesterol **15mg.**
Total fat **16g.**
Saturated fat **4g.**
Sodium **195mg.**

1¼ cups unbleached all-purpose flour
½ tsp. salt
3 tbsp. vegetable shortening
6 oz. beef tenderloin, cut into 1-by-1½-inch pieces
½ tbsp. virgin olive oil
½ head crisp lettuce, leaves washed, dried, and shredded
¼ sweet green pepper, seeded, deribbed, and chopped
¼ sweet red pepper, seeded, deribbed, and chopped
¼ sweet yellow pepper, seeded, deribbed, and chopped
¼ cucumber, halved lengthwise and sliced
2 scallions, sliced
5 black olives, pitted and sliced
3 tomatoes, cut into thin wedges

Chili and lime marinade

1 green chili pepper, finely chopped (cautionary note, page 18)
1 lime, juice strained and zest grated
1 garlic clove, finely chopped
½ tbsp. virgin olive oil
freshly ground black pepper

Chili and lime vinaigrette

1 green chili pepper, finely chopped (cautionary note, page 18)
1½ tbsp. fresh lime juice
½ tsp. tomato paste
½ tbsp. red wine vinegar
3 tbsp. virgin olive oil
1 tsp. finely chopped fresh oregano, or ½ tsp. dried oregano
¼ tsp. salt
freshly ground black pepper

First, make the tortillas. Mix the flour with the salt and rub in the vegetable shortening. Gradually add about 6 tablespoons of warm water and knead the mixture into a dough for about one minute. Add a little more flour if the dough is sticky, or water if it is too dry. Let the dough rest for 15 to 20 minutes, then divide it into four, and roll out each piece on a floured work surface to make a circle that is 10 inches in diameter and about ⅛ inch thick. Heat a lightly oiled crepe or frying pan, and fry each tortilla until bubbles form and the surface is slightly speckled—about 30 seconds. Flatten the bubbles with a wooden spatula, then turn the tortilla over and cook for another 30 seconds. Set the cooked tortillas aside.

Preheat the oven to 350° F.

To make the marinade, mix the chili pepper, lime juice and zest, garlic, oil, and some pepper together in a shallow bowl. Add the beef, turn the pieces to coat them, and let them marinate for 15 to 20 minutes. Prepare the vinaigrette by mixing the chili pepper, lime juice, tomato paste, vinegar, oil, oregano, salt, and some pepper together in a small bowl.

Heat the olive oil in a nonstick frying pan over medium heat. Pat the meat dry with a paper towel and sauté it for two to three minutes. While the meat cooks, place the tortillas in the oven for two to three minutes to reheat; they will dry out if left any longer.

Remove the meat from the pan, and mix it in a bowl with the lettuce, sweet peppers, cucumber, scallions, olives, and tomatoes; pour in the vinaigrette and toss the salad ingredients. Cut the tortillas in half. Fold each tortilla half into a cornet shape and fill it with some of the salad mixture. Serve immediately, while the tortillas and beef are still warm.

Chicken and Orange Pitas

Serves 6
Working (and total) time: about 15 minutes

Calories **180**
Protein **18g.**
Cholesterol **50mg.**
Total fat **7g.**
Saturated fat **1g.**
Sodium **230mg.**

2 oranges
12 oz. cooked chicken breast, diced
½ head small crisp lettuce, leaves washed, dried, and torn into bite-size pieces
3 whole-wheat pitas
Watercress dressing
½ bunch watercress (3 oz.), washed and dried, thick stems removed
2 tbsp. mayonnaise
2 tbsp. plain low-fat yogurt
¼ tsp. salt
freshly ground black pepper

Preheat the oven to 400° F. To make the dressing, put the watercress, mayonnaise, yogurt, salt, and some pepper into a blender or a food processor, and purée for a few seconds until smooth. Set the dressing aside.

Cut away the peel, white pith, and outer membrane from the oranges. To separate the segments from the inner membranes, slice down to the core with a sharp knife on either side of each segment; cut each segment in half. Place the chicken, lettuce, and orange segments in a bowl, and mix together.

Warm the pitas in the oven until they puff up—about one minute. Cut them in half, then open up each half to form a pocket; stuff the pitas with the chicken mixture. Spoon generous amounts of watercress dressing into each pita and serve immediately.

Creamed Mushrooms on Toast

Serves 2
Working (and total) time: about 15 minutes

Calories **150**
Protein **5g.**
Cholesterol **10mg.**
Total fat **5g.**
Saturated fat **2g.**
Sodium **400mg.**

2 slices whole-grain bread
½ cup unsalted chicken or vegetable stock (recipes, page 139)
1 tbsp. Madeira
1 tsp. fresh lemon juice
6 oz. mushrooms, wiped clean
2 tbsp. sour cream
¼ tsp. salt
freshly ground black pepper
½ tsp. Dijon mustard
½ tsp. mustard seeds
watercress leaves for garnish

Toast the bread slices on one side only and set aside.

Pour the stock, Madeira, and lemon juice into a shallow saucepan, cover, and bring to a boil. Lower the heat, add the mushrooms, and simmer them for about four minutes. With a slotted spoon, remove the mushrooms and set them aside. Then, to reduce the cooking liquid, place the pan over high heat and boil until about 2 tablespoons remain. Add the sour cream to the liquid and reduce for a few seconds. Return the mushrooms to the liquid, warm through, and season with the salt, some pepper, and the mustard. Preheat the broiler.

Pour the mixture onto the untoasted side of the bread, sprinkle with the mustard seeds, and place under the broiler until the seeds pop—about 20 seconds. Serve at once, garnished with the watercress.

Seafood and Asparagus Muffins

Serves 4
Working (and total) time: about 30 minutes

Calories **180**
Protein **15g.**
Cholesterol **50mg.**
Total fat **8g.**
Saturated fat **4g.**
Sodium **365mg.**

4 asparagus spears, trimmed and peeled
16 fresh mussels, scrubbed and debearded
2 tbsp. unsalted butter, softened
2 tsp. tomato paste
1 tbsp. finely chopped fresh dill
2 whole-wheat English muffins
4 oz. peeled, cooked crayfish or medium shrimp

Cook the asparagus in boiling water until it is tender—three to four minutes—then drain it in a colander and refresh under cold running water. Drain well. Cut off the tips, leaving them whole, and dice the stalks. Set the asparagus aside.

Pour 4 tablespoons of water into a large pan. Add the mussels, cover the pan, and bring the water to a boil. Steam the mussels until their shells open—four to five minutes. Let the mussels cool in their liquid, then remove them from the pan, discarding any that remain closed. Using your fingers or the edge of a spoon, detach the flesh from the shells. Set the mussels aside. Preheat the broiler.

Mix the butter, tomato paste, and dill, blending them well. Split the muffins and toast them until they are lightly browned. Spread the muffins with about half of the tomato butter, then divide the asparagus, mussels, and crayfish or shrimp among the muffins. Melt the remaining tomato butter and brush it over the top of the seafood. Broil the muffins for three to four minutes to heat them through, and serve at once.

Baked Oysters

Makes 12 oysters
Working time: about 30 minutes
Total time: about 40 minutes

Per oyster:
Calories **45**
Protein **5g.**
Cholesterol **20mg.**
Total fat **2g.**
Saturated fat **1g.**
Sodium **190mg.**

12 oz. spinach, washed and stemmed
1 tbsp. unsalted butter
6 scallions, trimmed and finely sliced
freshly ground black pepper
12 fresh oysters
coarse salt for baking
Parmesan topping
1 oz. Parmesan cheese, finely grated
2 tbsp. fresh whole-wheat breadcrumbs
1 tbsp. finely chopped parsley

Preheat the oven to 425° F.

Plunge the spinach into a saucepan of boiling water, bring the water back to a boil, and cook for 30 seconds. Drain the spinach in a colander and refresh it under cold running water. Squeeze the spinach dry, then finely chop it.

Heat the butter in a frying pan, then add the scallions and cook them over medium-low heat until they are soft—two to three minutes. Stir in the spinach and cook for three to four minutes, stirring frequently. Season with some black pepper.

To make the topping, mix the cheese, breadcrumbs, and parsley together. Open the oysters *(technique, below)* and discard their flat half shells. With the oysters on their rounder half shells, divide the spinach mixture equally among them, spooning it neatly on top. Sprinkle the topping evenly over the oysters.

Pour coarse salt into a large, ovenproof dish to a depth of about 1 inch. Place the oysters on the bed of salt and bake in the oven until they are golden brown—10 to 15 minutes. Serve warm.

Shucking an Oyster

1 *OPENING THE SHELL. Scrub the oyster well. Place it on a work surface with its rounder side down to catch the liquid. Grip the oyster with a towel to protect your hand, leaving the hinged end exposed, and force the tip of an oyster knife or other broad blade into the hinge. Twist the blade to pry the shells apart.*

2 *FREEING THE OYSTER. Sliding the knife blade along the inside of the upper shell, sever the muscle that attaches the flesh to the shell. Discard the upper shell, then slide the blade under the oyster to free it .*

Goat Cheese on Toast

Serves 4
Working time: about 30 minutes
Total time: about 12 hours and 30 minutes
(includes marinating)

Calories **180**
Protein **8g.**
Cholesterol **20mg.**
Total fat **11g.**
Saturated fat **4g.**
Sodium **370mg.**

2 small goat cheeses (about 3½ oz. total weight)
2 tbsp. virgin olive oil
½ tsp. crushed black peppercorns
1 bay leaf
1 garlic clove, crushed
1 tbsp. finely chopped fresh herbs, such as chives, tarragon, or rosemary
4 thin slices French bread, cut diagonally
½ cup fresh breadcrumbs
assorted salad greens

Remove the thin layer of rind on the cheeses and cut each cheese into four rounds. Mix the oil, peppercorns, bay leaf, garlic, and herbs in a bowl, and add the cheese rounds. Turn them to coat them well, then marinate them in the refrigerator for about 12 hours.

Preheat the oven to 350° F.

Put the slices of bread in the oven for about four minutes, then brush them with the marinade. Increase the oven temperature to 475° F.

Remove the cheese slices from the marinade and dip them in the breadcrumbs, pressing lightly to make the crumbs adhere. Place two cheese slices on top of each toast, and return them to the oven until the toast is slightly brown and the cheese softened—about 10 minutes. Serve the hot toasts immediately, accompanied by the salad leaves.

EDITOR'S NOTE: *The marinade may be reserved and used to dress the salad leaves, but this will increase the calorie and fat content of the snack.*

Tuna Tapenade Pizzas

IN THIS RECIPE, TUNA FISH REPLACES A LARGE PERCENTAGE
OF THE OILY INGREDIENTS OF THE TRADITIONAL PROVENÇAL
TAPENADE—AN OIL, OLIVE, AND ANCHOVY PURÉE.

Serves 6
Working time: about 40 minutes
Total time: about 2 hours (includes proofing)

Calories **340**
Protein **14g.**
Cholesterol **25mg.**
Total fat **15g.**
Saturated fat **2g.**
Sodium **305mg.**

1 envelope (¼ oz.) active dry yeast
2½ cups unbleached all-purpose flour
1 tsp. salt
1 tbsp. virgin olive oil
6 cherry tomatoes, sliced, for garnish
chopped parsley for garnish (optional)
Tuna tapenade
3 anchovy fillets, rinsed, dried, and finely chopped
1 garlic clove, finely chopped
1½ tbsp. capers, finely chopped
12 black olives, pitted and finely chopped
7 oz. tuna fish packed in water, drained
1 tbsp. virgin olive oil
freshly ground black pepper

Mix the yeast with ⅓ cup of tepid water and let it stand
until it is frothy—10 to 15 minutes. Sift the flour and
salt into a large bowl, and make a well in the flour. Pour

the yeast mixture into the well along with the oil, and
mix in enough tepid water to make a soft but not sticky
dough. On a floured work surface, knead the dough
until it is smooth and elastic—about 10 minutes—then
gather the dough into a ball and leave it in a clean
bowl, covered with plastic wrap, until it has doubled
in volume—about one hour.

Preheat the oven to 425° F.

Lightly oil a baking sheet. Punch the dough down to
deflate it, then divide it into six balls. On a floured work
surface, roll out each ball into a 5-inch-diameter circle.
Press the edges of the circles to create a raised rim,
then put them on the baking tray and let them rise a
little—at least 10 minutes.

To make the *tapenade,* pound the anchovies and
garlic together in a mortar. Add the capers, olives,
tuna, oil, and some pepper in gradual stages, continuing to pound to form a paste. You may also blend
the *tapenade* in a food processor. Divide the paste
equally among the pizza crusts and spread it to within
¼ inch of the edges. Bake the pizzas in the oven for
15 minutes, then garnish them with the tomato slices
and return to the oven for a final five minutes.

Serve warm, garnished with a little chopped parsley,
if you wish.

SUGGESTED ACCOMPANIMENT: *leafy salad.*

Calzone

THE DOUGH AND INGREDIENTS OF CALZONE ARE SIMILAR
TO THOSE OF PIZZA; INSTEAD OF AN OPEN PIE, THE
DOUGH IS FOLDED OVER TO ENCLOSE THE FILLING. THE SHAPE
OF CALZONE DIFFERS FROM ONE REGION OF ITALY
TO ANOTHER—CRESCENTS, SQUARES, AND TRIANGLES ARE
ALL TO BE FOUND.

Makes 10 calzone
Working time: about 40 minutes
Total time: about 2 hours (includes proofing)

Per calzone:
Calories **255**
Protein **11g.**
Cholesterol **15mg.**
Total fat **6g.**
Saturated fat **3g.**
Sodium **400mg.**

1 envelope (¼ oz.) active dry yeast
4 cups unbleached all-purpose flour, sifted
1½ tsp. salt
1 tbsp. virgin olive oil
1 lb. large tomatoes, peeled, seeded (technique, page 76), and chopped
1 tbsp. tomato paste
1 tsp. dried oregano
freshly ground black pepper
6 oz. low-fat mozzarella cheese, sliced
2 oz. prosciutto, chopped

Mix the yeast with ⅓ cup of tepid water and let it stand
until it is frothy—10 to 15 minutes. Sift the flour and
salt into a bowl, and make a well in the center. Pour
in the yeast mixture, and mix in enough tepid water to

make a soft but not sticky dough. Turn the dough onto
a floured surface, and knead until it is smooth and
elastic—about 10 minutes. Return the dough to the
bowl, cover with plastic wrap, and let it rise in a warm
place until doubled in volume—about one hour.

To make the filling, heat the oil in a small pan over
medium heat, add the tomatoes and tomato paste,
and cook for about five minutes. Stir in the oregano,
the remaining salt, and some pepper, then allow the
filling to cool.

Preheat the oven to 425° F.

Turn the dough onto a floured surface, knead for a
few minutes, then divide it into 10 pieces. Roll out each
piece into a rectangle approximately 4 by 8 inches.
Spread the tomato mixture over one-half of each rectangle, leaving a small border; reserve any tomato
juices in the pan. Top the tomato mixture with the
mozzarella and prosciutto, then dampen the edges of
the dough, fold the dough over the filling, and press
the edges together to seal them. Arrange the calzone
on a lightly oiled baking sheet and brush them with the
reserved tomato juices. Cover the calzone with oiled
plastic wrap and let them rise for 10 minutes.

Bake the calzone in the oven until they are puffed
up and golden—8 to 10 minutes. Serve hot.

SUGGESTED ACCOMPANIMENT: *leafy salad.*

Herb Focaccia

FOCACCIA IS A GENOESE BREAD MADE WITH OLIVE OIL. HERE, ONE LOAF HAS A TOMATO AND BRESAOLA TOPPING; THE OTHER LOAF IS SERVED PLAIN.

Serves 12
Working time: about 45 minutes
Total time: about 2 hours and 15 minutes
(includes proofing)

Calories **260**
Protein **8g.**
Cholesterol **5mg.**
Total fat **5g.**
Saturated fat **1g.**
Sodium **125mg.**

2 envelopes (½ oz.) active dry yeast
7 cups unbleached all-purpose flour
¾ tsp. salt
3 tbsp. virgin olive oil
6 leaves fresh sage, finely chopped
1 tbsp. finely chopped rosemary leaves
1 tbsp. chopped fresh oregano or marjoram
2 tbsp. chopped or torn basil leaves
12 green olives, pitted and finely chopped
2 tbsp. chopped rosemary, sage, or basil leaves
2 large tomatoes, thinly sliced
1 oz. bresaola or prosciutto, cut into strips

Mix the yeast with ¾ cup of tepid water and let it stand until it is frothy—10 to 15 minutes. Sift the flour with ½ teaspoon of the salt, make a well in the center, and pour in 2 tablespoons of the olive oil and 1 cup of tepid water. Add the sage, rosemary, oregano or marjoram, basil, and olives, then the yeast solution. Gradually incorporate the flour into the liquid, and knead the dough until it is smooth and elastic—about 10 minutes. Form the dough into a ball and brush lightly with a little olive oil; place the dough in a large bowl, cover it with plastic wrap, and leave in a warm place to rise until it has doubled in volume—about one hour.

Brush two 9-by-12-inch cake pans with a little olive oil. Punch down the dough, and with floured hands, knead it for a minute or two on a lightly floured surface. Stretch and press the dough until it is about ¾ inch thick. Divide the dough in half and press it into the pans, pushing it hard into the corners.

Dimple the surface of the dough with your knuckles and brush it with the remaining olive oil. Sprinkle one pan of dough with the remaining salt; sprinkle the second pan with the 2 tablespoons of chopped rosemary, sage, or basil leaves, and arrange the tomato slices in rows over the top.

Preheat the oven to 450° F. Allow the dough to rise until it has almost doubled in volume—15 to 25 minutes. Bake the bread in the center of the oven until lightly golden—15 to 20 minutes. Remove the tomato-garnished *focaccia* from the oven, scatter the bresaola or prosciutto between the rows of tomato, and return it to the oven for just one minute. Remove both pans from the oven and transfer the bread to a wire rack. Cut each into 12 pieces; serve the bread warm.

Chicken and Walnut Pizzas

Serves 6
Working time: about 45 minutes
Total time: about 2 hours

Calories **365**
Protein **19g.**
Cholesterol **30mg.**
Total fat **15g.**
Saturated fat **3g.**
Sodium **180mg.**

3 chicken thighs (about 12 oz.)
1 carrot, coarsely chopped
1 large onion, coarsely chopped, plus 1 tsp. finely chopped onion
6 black peppercorns
1 sprig thyme
1 bay leaf
½ cup walnuts
1 garlic clove, finely chopped
⅛ tsp. cayenne pepper
⅛ tsp. paprika
¼ tsp. salt
½ sweet red pepper, cored, deribbed, seeded, and sliced into thin rings
parsley for garnish
Pizza dough
1 envelope (¼ oz.) active dry yeast
2¼ cups unbleached all-purpose flour
¼ tsp. salt
1 tbsp. virgin olive oil

First, make the pizza dough. Mix the yeast with ⅓ cup of tepid water and let it stand until it is frothy—10 to 15 minutes. Sift the flour and salt into a large bowl. Pour the yeast mixture into the bowl along with the oil, and mix in enough tepid water to make a soft but not sticky dough. On a floured work surface, knead the dough until it is smooth and elastic—about 10 minutes. Form the dough into a ball, then place it in a clean bowl, cover with plastic wrap, and set it aside until it has doubled in volume—about one hour.

While the dough is proofing, put the chicken thighs into a saucepan and pour in enough cold water to cover them. Add the carrot, coarsely chopped onion, peppercorns, thyme, and bay leaf. Bring to a boil, then lower the heat, cover, and simmer gently for 15 to 20 minutes. Take the pan off the heat and let it cool.

Preheat the oven to 425° F.

Lightly oil two baking sheets. Punch the dough down to deflate it, then divide it into six balls. On a floured work surface, roll out each ball into a 4-by-6-inch oval. Press up the edges to form raised rims, then put the ovals on the baking sheets and allow them to rise a little more.

Strain the stock from the saucepan and reserve it. Skin and bone the chicken thighs and coarsely chop the meat.

In a food processor, finely chop the walnuts, then mix in the finely chopped onion, the garlic, cayenne pepper, paprika, and salt. Add up to ⅔ cup of the reserved stock to make a smooth, pale sauce when thoroughly blended.

Divide the sauce among the pizza crusts and spread it to within ¼ inch of the edges. Bake the pizzas in the oven for 10 to 15 minutes. Sprinkle each one with the chopped chicken and a red-pepper ring, then return the pizzas to the oven for another 5 to 10 minutes. Serve warm, garnished with the parsley.

Scallop Galettes

Serves 8
Working time: about 45 minutes
Total time: about 1 hour

Calories **165**
Protein **9g.**
Cholesterol **50mg.**
Total fat **6g.**
Saturated fat **3g.**
Sodium **270mg.**

¾ cup buckwheat flour
⅓ cup unbleached all-purpose flour
¾ tsp. salt
2 tbsp. unsalted butter
1 tsp. honey
1 egg, lightly beaten
1 cup sparkling apple cider
1 lb. spinach, washed, stems removed
2 tbsp. sour cream
freshly ground black pepper
grated nutmeg
¼ tsp. safflower oil
8 scallops, bright white connective tissue removed, scallops rinsed

To make the galette batter, first sift both kinds of flour and ¼ teaspoon of the salt into a mixing bowl, and form a well in the center. Melt 1 tablespoon of the butter, and pour it into the well with ½ teaspoon of the honey, the egg, ½ cup of the cider, and ½ cup of water. Using a wooden spoon, gradually draw the dry ingredients into the liquids. Beat lightly until the mixture is free of lumps, then set the batter aside to rest for about 30 minutes.

Place the washed spinach with the water still clinging to its leaves in a large, heavy-bottomed saucepan. Cover the pan and steam the spinach over medium heat until the leaves are wilted—two to three minutes. Drain the spinach quickly, squeeze out all excess moisture, and coarsely chop it with a knife. Return the spinach to the saucepan, and stir in 1 tablespoon of the remaining cider and half the sour cream. Season with ¼ teaspoon of the salt and some pepper and nutmeg. Set the spinach mixture aside until you are ready to serve the galettes.

When the batter is ready, heat a 7-inch crepe or nonstick frying pan *(box, page 86)* over medium-high heat. Add the safflower oil and spread it over the entire surface with a paper towel. Put 2 to 3 tablespoons of the batter into the pan, and immediately swirl the pan to coat the bottom with a thin, even layer of batter. Cook until the bottom is lightly browned—about 30 seconds. Lift the edge with a spatula and turn the galette over. Cook it on the second side until that, too, is lightly browned. Slide the galette onto a heated plate. Repeat the process with the remaining batter, brushing the pan lightly with more oil if the galettes begin to stick. Stack the cooked galettes on the plate as you go, and then cover them with a dishtowel and set aside, or keep them warm in a 300° F. oven until all eight are cooked and ready to be filled.

Slice each scallop horizontally into two or three rounds. Melt the remaining butter in a heavy frying pan and toss the scallop slices in the butter until they are opaque—about two minutes. Add the remaining cider and cook over medium heat for 30 seconds more. Mix in the rest of the sour cream, honey, and salt, season with some nutmeg, and return the pan to the heat for a few seconds to heat through. Remove the pan from the heat. Reheat the spinach on medium, stirring continuously.

To serve, place a spoonful of spinach in the center of each galette, and arrange two or three scallop slices in each nest of spinach. Fold over the four rounded edges of each galette to form a small, square parcel, leaving the scallop slices partly exposed. Grind some pepper over the top, if you like, and serve immediately.

Spanish Tortilla Triangles

Serves 8
Working time: about 15 minutes
Total time: about 25 minutes

2 tbsp. virgin olive oil
2 leeks, trimmed, cleaned (technique, below), and cut diagonally into fine slices
2 garlic cloves, finely chopped
1 sweet red pepper, seeded, deribbed, and finely chopped
1 green pepper, seeded, deribbed, and finely chopped
4 eggs
½ tsp. salt
freshly ground black pepper
½ lb. cooked, peeled potatoes, chopped
2 tbsp. chopped parsley

Heat 1½ tablespoons of the oil in a heavy frying pan and cook the leeks over low heat until they are soft—about 10 minutes. Add the garlic and peppers, and cook for 10 minutes more, stirring occasionally.

Mix the eggs in a bowl with the salt and some pepper, then stir in the cooked vegetable mixture, potatoes, and parsley. Preheat the broiler.

Heat the remaining oil in a 9-inch omelet pan and pour in the egg mixture. Cook over low heat until the bottom of the omelet is golden brown—about four minutes. (Lift the omelet gently with a spatula to check.) Place the pan under the broiler and cook until the egg is set—about three minutes.

Slide the omelet onto a serving plate and cut into eight triangles. Serve immediately.

Cleaning Leeks

1 *SPLITTING THE LEEK. Remove any bruised outer leaves from the leek. Cut off the root base and the tough leaf tops. With a paring knife, pierce the leek about 2 inches below the green portion, then draw the knife through to the top to split the leek.*

2 *RINSING OUT THE GRIT. Dip the leafy part of the leek into a bowl of water and swirl it vigorously to flush out the grit. Alternatively, rinse the leek well under running water. Run your fingers along the insides of the leaves to remove any remaining particles of sand.*

4 Pita-bread pockets bulging with vegetables (recipe, opposite) provide a satisfying hot snack rich in vitamins and minerals.

Snacks from the Microwave

By their very nature, party foods and light snacks often call for speedy production, and it is in preparing them that a microwave oven truly earns its place in the busy kitchen. While retaining the healthful aspects of the preceding chapters, the recipes here are designed to capitalize on the microwave's abbreviated process. The dough for a pizza *(page 138)*, for example, can be proofed in just 20 minutes instead of the usual hour, while the potatoes in their skins on page 135 take only 10 minutes to cook—less than a quarter of the time they would require in a conventional oven. Furthermore, most of the dishes can be made in advance, then cooked or reheated at the last minute.

The microwave oven offers bonuses in addition to speed. Because vegetables spend a short time in the oven, with little or no added liquid, they cook in their own juices. As a result, few nutrients are lost, and the vegetables emerge with their natural color and texture intact. Moreover, food cooked in the microwave usually does not brown—except with the aid of a special browning dish. Although a microwave is generally unsuitable for traditional roasts and crusty gratins, this can be turned into an advantage. Low-calorie wrappers such as cabbage leaves *(page 130)* can be substituted for high-fat pastry without the risk of charring; bread-wrapped dishes, such as the ginger-stirred vegetables here, can be reheated without their cases drying out the way they might in a regular oven.

One caution: Some of these recipes call for the food to be covered with plastic wrap, but use only wrap that is microwave safe. And if you are covering a dish containing liquid, leave a corner of the wrap open or slit it with a knife to avoid a dangerous steam buildup.

All of the recipes have been tested in 625- and 700-watt ovens. But since power settings vary among ovens made by different manufacturers, the term "high" is used here to indicate 100 percent power, "medium" for 70 percent, and "low" for 30 percent. Because it is easy to overcook food in the microwave, always use the shortest time specified.

Ginger-Stirred Vegetables in Pita

Serves 4
Working (and total) time: about 20 minutes

Calories **165**
Protein **5g.**
Cholesterol **0mg.**
Total fat **5g.**
Saturated fat **1g.**
Sodium **390mg.**

2 large pitas, or 4 small pitas
1 tbsp. light sesame oil
1 small garlic clove, crushed
2 pieces fresh ginger (about 1 inch each), peeled
2 oz. fresh shiitake mushrooms, sliced, or 1 oz. dried shiitake mushrooms, covered with hot water and soaked for 20 minutes, drained, and sliced
4 canned or frozen baby corn, sliced
3 medium zucchini, julienned
1 tbsp. fresh lemon juice
1 tsp. tamari, or 1 tsp. low-sodium soy sauce mixed with ½ tsp. honey
¼ tsp. salt
freshly ground black pepper

Wrap the pitas in paper towels, and microwave on high for 30 seconds. If you are using large pitas, cut them in half crosswise; if you are using small pitas, cut them open along one side.

Place the oil and garlic in a wide, shallow dish. Using a garlic press, squeeze the juice from one piece of ginger, and shred the second piece very finely. Add the ginger juice and shreds to the oil.

Microwave the oil and flavorings on high for 30 seconds. Add the mushrooms to the dish, cover with plastic wrap, leaving a corner open, and cook on medium for two minutes. Add the corn, re-cover the dish, leaving a corner open as before, and cook for 20 seconds more on medium. Then add the zucchini to the mushrooms and corn, and cook, uncovered, on high for one minute.

Season with the lemon juice, tamari or soy sauce, salt, and a few generous grindings of black pepper, and divide the mixture among the pita pockets.

Arrange the pitas on paper towels or a serving dish in a single layer, evenly spaced. Microwave on medium for one and a half minutes, rearranging the pitas halfway through that time to ensure even cooking.

Serve at once.

Vegetable Tartlets

Makes 8 tartlets
Working (and total) time: about 40 minutes

Per tartlet:
Calories **100**
Protein **7g.**
Cholesterol **35mg.**
Total fat **5g.**
Saturated fat **2g.**
Sodium **160mg.**

8 small leaves savoy cabbage
2 medium zucchini, finely shredded
1 medium carrot, peeled and finely grated
1 tbsp. fresh lemon juice
⅔ cup low-fat cottage cheese
1 egg yolk
2 tbsp. plain low-fat yogurt
½ tsp. dry mustard
1 tbsp. unbleached all-purpose flour
1 tsp. ground cinnamon
1 tbsp. chopped fresh basil
½ oz. feta cheese, crumbled
1 tsp. finely chopped mint, plus 8 mint sprigs for garnish

Blanch the cabbage leaves in a saucepan of lightly salted boiling water until they are pliable but still firm—three to five minutes. Drain them, rinse the leaves under cold running water, then dry them thoroughly on paper towels. Cut away any hard central ribs, and use each leaf to line a microwave muffin mold or ramekin. Using kitchen scissors, trim the edges of the leaves so they rise no more than 1 inch above the rim of the molds.

Place the zucchini in a shallow dish and cover them with plastic wrap, leaving a corner open. Microwave on high for three minutes, stirring twice during this time. Drain in a fine sieve. Place the grated carrot in the dish with a few drops of the lemon juice, and cover the dish with plastic wrap, again leaving a corner open. Microwave on high for two minutes, then set aside. If the cottage cheese is chilled, soften it a little by microwaving on low for about 45 seconds.

In a mixing bowl, beat the cottage cheese with the egg yolk until the mixture is thoroughly blended. In another bowl, mix together the yogurt and remaining lemon juice, blend in the mustard and flour, and stir until no lumps remain. Add this mixture to the cottage cheese and beat gently but thoroughly. Squeeze the drained zucchini to remove any remaining liquid, then add the zucchini, carrots, cinnamon, and basil to the cheese mixture. Stir well. Divide the mixture among the eight lined molds, and sprinkle a little of the feta cheese and chopped mint on top of each.

Arrange the molds in the microwave oven, making sure they are evenly spaced; a circle of molds would be ideal. Microwave on medium low for eight minutes, rearranging the molds every two minutes. Let them stand for two minutes, then check that the centers are fairly firm to the touch. If they are not, cook for two minutes more on low and test again. If necessary, cook the tartlets for a final two minutes on low, then remove them from the oven; let the tartlets rest for a minute or two to firm up the centers.

Serve the tartlets warm or at room temperature, garnished with the mint sprigs.

Vegetable Purées in Endive

Makes about 50 leaves
Working time: about 40 minutes
Total time: about 1 hour

4 medium carrots, peeled and coarsely sliced
1 orange, grated zest of half, juice of whole
12 oz. Brussels sprouts, trimmed
3 medium potatoes, scrubbed well, dried, and pricked all over with a fork
½ cup sour cream
1 tsp. ground coriander
ground white pepper
¾ tsp. salt
1 tbsp. hazelnut or walnut oil
¼ tsp. grated nutmeg
1 small bunch parsley, chopped
4 heads Belgian endive

Place the carrots and the orange zest and juice in a dish. Cover the dish with plastic wrap, leaving one corner open, and microwave on high until the carrots are tender—about eight minutes. Set aside to cool.

Place the Brussels sprouts and 4 tablespoons of water in another dish. Cover the dish with plastic wrap, leaving one corner open, and microwave on high until the sprouts are soft—six to eight minutes. Set aside.

Arrange the potatoes, evenly spaced on paper towels, in the oven. Microwave on high for about 10 minutes, turning them over halfway through cooking. Let them rest for two minutes; if they are not soft, microwave for two to five minutes more. Let them cool, then remove the skins.

In a food processor or a blender, process the carrots until they are finely chopped. Add 2 tablespoons of the sour cream, the coriander, some white pepper, and ¼ teaspoon of the salt, and blend until puréed.

Remove the carrot purée from the processor and clean the bowl. Process the sprouts until they are finely chopped, then add the oil, nutmeg, and ¼ teaspoon of the salt, and blend again until puréed. Add 1½ tablespoons of the sour cream and blend to form a very smooth purée. Mash the potatoes, then beat them with the parsley and the remaining sour cream and salt until the mixture is soft and smooth.

Separate the Belgian-endive leaves, and wash and dry them carefully.

Using a pastry bag fitted with a large star tip, fill one-third of the endive leaves with the carrot purée, one-third with the sprout purée, and one-third with the potato purée. Arrange them on a platter and serve.

Spiced Coconut Crab Dip with Poppadoms

Serves 8
Working (and total) time: about 30 minutes

Calories **140**
Protein **9g.**
Cholesterol **30mg.**
Total fat **5g.**
Saturated fat **1g.**
Sodium **260mg.**

2 oz. cream of coconut
1 cup unsalted chicken stock (recipe, page 139)
1-inch piece fresh ginger, peeled and sliced
6 cardamom pods, crushed
¼ tsp. ground mace
2 chili peppers, split lengthwise and seeded (cautionary note, page 18)
½ tsp. ground turmeric
⅛ tsp. saffron threads
1 bay leaf
5 tbsp. sour cream
2 tsp. cornstarch
1 tsp. dry mustard
2 tbsp. dry sherry
1 tbsp. tomato paste
½ lb. white crabmeat, picked over
1 tamarillo, peeled, seeded, and finely diced (optional)
1 tsp. fresh lemon juice
½ tsp. salt
¼ tsp. cayenne pepper, plus a sprinkling for garnish
16 poppadoms
finely shredded chili pepper for garnish

Blend the cream of coconut with the chicken stock in a bowl. Add the ginger, cardamom, mace, chilies, turmeric, saffron, and bay leaf. Microwave on low for five minutes to infuse the liquid with the spices. Strain the coconut mixture through a sieve into a 1-quart dish, pressing down hard on the spices. Stir in the sour cream and mix well.

In a small bowl, blend the cornstarch, dry mustard, and sherry, and stir this into the coconut mixture. Then stir in the tomato paste. Microwave the mixture on medium until the liquid has thickened and begun to bubble—about three minutes. Stir the crabmeat into the mixture, and microwave for 30 seconds on medium. Stir in the tamarillo, if you are using it, and microwave for 30 seconds more, again on medium. Add the lemon juice, salt, and cayenne pepper.

Place four poppadoms at a time in the oven in a single layer on sheets of paper towels, and cook on high for about one minute, rearranging after 30 seconds; the poppadoms are cooked when they appear evenly "puffed" and no dark patches remain.

While the poppadoms are cooking, transfer the dip to a serving dish, and garnish with a little shredded chili and a sprinkling of cayenne pepper. Serve the dip with the poppadoms as soon as they are ready.

EDITOR'S NOTE: *Poppadoms—partially prepared flat bread— are available in Indian markets and many supermarkets.*

Spinach and Salmon Canapés

Makes 12 canapés
Working time: about 25 minutes
Total time: about 30 minutes

Per canapé:
Calories **90**
Protein **9g.**
Cholesterol **25mg.**
Total fat **4g.**
Saturated fat **1g.**
Sodium **140mg.**

½ *lb. salmon steak, skinned and boned*
2 egg whites
6 oz. skinned sole or turbot fillets
2 tbsp. plain low-fat yogurt
1 small sweet red pepper, pricked all over with a fork
6 oz. spinach leaves, stemmed, washed, and drained
6 slices whole-wheat bread
curly endive for garnish (optional)

Finely chop the salmon in a food processor, then blend in one egg white. Transfer the mixture to a bowl. Repeat this procedure with the sole or turbot and the second egg white. Stir 1 tablespoon of the yogurt into each of the mixtures and chill them.

Place the red pepper on a paper towel in the microwave oven, and microwave on high for four minutes, turning after every minute. Put the pepper into a small bowl, cover with plastic wrap, and let it cool.

Peel off the skin and remove the seeds, then cut out 12 small diamond shapes from the flesh. Set aside.

Put the spinach leaves into a bowl, cover, and microwave on high for four minutes. Drain the spinach well, taking care not to break up the leaves.

Line the hollows of two plastic egg cartons with plastic wrap. Divide the sole or turbot mixture equally among the 12 molds, and smooth the surface. Divide the spinach into 12 portions and arrange each in an even layer over the sole. Top the spinach with an even layer of the salmon mixture. Cook one box at a time on high until the fish mixtures are just firm to the touch—one and a half to two minutes.

Meanwhile, toast the bread and cut out 12 circles with a 1¾-inch round cutter.

Put a plate over each carton and invert it to remove the fish molds; drain off any liquid. Lift each mold onto a circle of toast and place a red-pepper diamond on top. Arrange the canapés on a plate, garnish with the curly endive if you wish, and serve them warm.

EDITOR'S NOTE: *If you wish to serve the canapés cold, let the fish molds cool in the egg cartons, then place them on the circles of toast just before serving. Small egg cups may be used in place of egg cartons to cook the fish molds. The unused pepper may be sliced and used in a salad or puréed for a sauce.*

Peanut and Spinach Pinwheels

Makes 16 pinwheels
Working time: about 20 minutes
Total time: about 1 hour and 20 minutes (includes chilling)

Per pinwheel:
Calories **45**
Protein **3g.**
Cholesterol **30mg.**
Total fat **3g.**
Saturated fat **1g.**
Sodium **20mg.**

½ cup unsalted dry-roasted peanuts
2 eggs
¼ cup unbleached all-purpose flour
¼ tsp. salt
freshly ground black pepper
4 oz. spinach, washed and stemmed
1 tsp. cornstarch
6 tbsp. skim milk
1 tsp. fresh lemon juice
⅛ tsp. grated nutmeg

Cut out a 9-inch square of parchment paper. Fold up the edges to form a shallow lip, and place the parchment on a microwave oven tray.

In a food processor, finely grind the peanuts. Break the eggs into a mixing bowl, and whisk until they are thick and frothy. Fold just over half of the peanuts into the eggs along with the flour, salt, and some pepper. Pour the mixture into the prepared parchment and gently spread it into an even layer. Cook on high for

two and a half to three minutes, turning the tray half a turn after one minute. The center should feel firm to the touch.

Turn out the cooked peanut mixture onto a sheet of parchment paper, remove the top parchment paper, and cover the mixture with a new piece of damp parchment. Roll it up like a jelly roll, with the damp parchment inside, and let it cool.

Put the spinach into a casserole dish. Cover the dish and cook on high for three minutes. Drain the spinach thoroughly, squeezing out as much water as possible, then chop it.

In a bowl, mix the cornstarch into a paste with a little of the milk, then blend in the remaining milk. Heat on high for one minute, then stir. Stir the spinach into the sauce. Season with the lemon juice, nutmeg, and a few grindings of black pepper.

Carefully unroll the roulade and remove the parchment paper. Spread the spinach mixture evenly over the surface, then reroll. Sprinkle the remaining ground peanuts on a piece of wax paper, and roll the roulade in them to coat the exterior. Wrap the roulade in wax paper and chill for about one hour. To serve, remove the paper and cut the roulade into 16 slices.

Leek and Bacon Potatoes

Serves 4
Working time: about 15 minutes
Total time: about 25 minutes

Calories **145**
Protein **8g.**
Cholesterol **10mg.**
Total fat **2g.**
Saturated fat **trace**
Sodium **340mg.**

4 potatoes (about 4 oz. each), scrubbed well, dried, and pricked all over with a fork
2 oz. Canadian bacon, trimmed of fat and diced
2 medium leeks, trimmed, cleaned (technique, page 127), and finely chopped
1 tbsp. skim milk
freshly ground black pepper

Place the potatoes in a circle on a paper towel in the microwave oven. Cook the potatoes on high for 10 minutes, turning them over after five minutes, then remove them from the oven and set them aside.

Put the bacon and leeks into a small bowl, and microwave on high for three minutes, stirring once.

Cut the tops off the potatoes and scoop out the insides to within ¼ inch of the skins. Mash the scooped-out potatoes with the milk and season with some pepper. Stir in the bacon and leeks. Pile the mashed-potato mixture back into the skins, place the lids on top, and reheat on high for one to two minutes before serving.

Glazed Chicken Drumsticks

Makes 6 drumsticks
Working (and total) time: about 30 minutes

Calories **130**
Protein **14g.**
Cholesterol **25mg.**
Total fat **6g.**
Saturated fat **2g.**
Sodium **115mg.**

1 tbsp. honey
1 tbsp. molasses
1 tbsp. low-sodium soy sauce
1 tbsp. cider vinegar
1 tbsp. tomato paste
1 small garlic clove, crushed
1-inch piece fresh ginger, peeled and finely chopped
½ tsp. ground cardamom
½ tbsp. Dijon mustard
¼ tsp. salt
⅛ tsp. cayenne pepper
1 tsp. ground arrowroot dissolved in 1½ tsp. water
6 chicken drumsticks (about 12 oz.), skinned
parsley sprigs for garnish

To prepare the glaze, place the honey, molasses, soy sauce, vinegar, tomato paste, crushed garlic, chopped ginger, cardamom, mustard, salt, and cayenne pepper in a bowl, and add 5 tablespoons of water. Microwave the mixture on high for four minutes, let it stand for two minutes, then strain it through a fine sieve, pressing down hard on the spices. Stir in the arrowroot, then return the bowl to the oven. Cook on high for one to one and a half minutes, stirring every 20 seconds, until the glaze becomes thick and clear.

Turn the drumsticks in the warm glaze to coat them thoroughly. Arrange them in a shallow dish in a wagon-wheel pattern, thin ends to the center; reserve the glaze. Microwave the drumsticks on high for two minutes, then turn them over, and give the dish a quarter turn. Cook for two minutes more, then turn the pieces, give the dish another quarter turn, and pour the reserved glaze over the chicken. Reduce the power to low and cook for four minutes more, giving the dish another quarter turn halfway through the cooking time.

Let the chicken rest for four minutes, then check for doneness by inserting a thin skewer into the thickest drumstick—the skewer should encounter virtually no resistance. Now grasp the bone and see if it will move slightly within the flesh—if it does, the chicken is cooked. If it is not cooked through, microwave on medium for two minutes more and let the drumsticks rest for two minutes before testing again.

Arrange the drumsticks on a serving plate and spoon the glaze over them. Garnish with the parsley sprigs.

EDITOR'S NOTE: *The drumsticks may be left to marinate overnight in the glaze before they are cooked. If you wish to serve them cold, let them cool in the glaze.*

Pineapple Chunks Wrapped in Spicy Beef

Makes about 40 chunks
Working time: about 20 minutes
Total time: about 1 hour and 20 minutes
(includes marinating)

Per chunk:
Calories **20**
Protein **3g.**
Cholesterol **10mg.**
Total fat **1g.**
Saturated fat **trace**
Sodium **5mg.**

12 oz. beef tenderloin
2 tbsp. sesame oil
2 tbsp. low-sodium soy sauce
1 garlic clove, crushed
½ tsp. chili powder
1 pineapple

Cut the beef across the grain into very thin slices. Cut the slices in half lengthwise, then stretch the pieces with the back of the knife to create strips approximately 3 by ½ inches.

Put the oil, soy sauce, garlic, and chili powder into a bowl. Stir in the beef slices to coat them well with the sauce. Cover the dish with plastic wrap and let the meat marinate for one hour, stirring twice.

Cut the top and bottom off the pineapple. Cut away the skin and slice the flesh into rings about ¾ inch thick. Remove the core from each slice and cut about 40 cubes from the slices.

Wrap a piece of beef around each pineapple chunk, and thread the chunks onto a cocktail stick. Arrange half of the wrapped chunks on a plate, so that they are evenly spaced around the outside, with their sticks pointing toward the center. Cook on high for two minutes, turning them over gently every 30 seconds. Let them rest for five minutes while you cook the second batch in the same way, then serve.

EDITOR'S NOTE: *The chunks may also be served chilled.*

Vegetable Whole-Wheat Pizza

Serves 4
Working time: about 25 minutes
Total time: about 45 minutes

Calories **250**
Protein **12g.**
Cholesterol **10mg.**
Total fat **9g.**
Saturated fat **3g.**
Sodium **420mg.**

¾ tsp. active dry yeast
1½ cups whole-wheat flour
¼ tsp. salt
1 tbsp. polyunsaturated margarine
3 tomatoes, quartered
1 small onion, chopped
1 tsp. virgin olive oil
freshly ground black pepper
1 zucchini, sliced
1 small sweet red pepper, cut into rings
4 frozen baby corn, unthawed
2 oz. mushrooms, sliced
1 tsp. dried oregano
2 oz. low-fat mozzarella, grated (about ¼ cup)

Mix the yeast with ½ cup of tepid water and let it stand for 10 minutes. Sift the flour and ⅛ teaspoon of the salt into a bowl, adding the bran left in the sieve. Rub in the margarine, then make a well in the center; pour the yeast into the well and mix it in with a wooden spoon, adding more water if necessary, to make a dough that can be formed into a ball.

Turn the dough out onto a lightly floured surface, and knead until it is smooth and elastic—5 to 10 minutes. Put the dough into a bowl, cover it with plastic wrap, and microwave on high for 10 seconds only. Let it stand for 10 minutes, then microwave on high for 10 seconds more and let it rise for 10 minutes; it should double in volume.

Meanwhile, cook the vegetables. Place the tomatoes on a plate. Microwave on high for one to two minutes, then remove the skins and chop the flesh. Put the onion into a small bowl with ½ teaspoon of the oil, and microwave on high for two minutes. Add the tomatoes, and season with the remaining salt and some pepper. Set aside.

Put the zucchini, the sweet red-pepper rings, baby corn, and mushrooms into a small bowl with 1 tablespoon of water; cover the bowl with plastic wrap, leaving one corner open, and microwave on high for three minutes. Drain the vegetables in a colander.

Turn the dough out onto a floured surface and knead lightly for one minute, then roll it out into a 10-inch circle. Brush a flat 10-inch-diameter plate with the remaining oil and place the dough on the plate. Spread the tomato and onion mixture over the dough, then arrange the other vegetables over the top of the tomatoes. Sprinkle the oregano and mozzarella over the vegetables. Proof the pizza by microwaving on high for 10 seconds, then let it rest for five minutes. Cook on high for five to six minutes. Let it rest for five minutes more before serving.

Chicken Stock

Makes about 2 quarts
Working time: about 20 minutes
Total time: about 3 hours

4 to 5 lb. uncooked chicken trimmings and bones (preferably wings, necks, and backs), the bones cracked with a heavy knife
2 carrots, peeled and cut into ½-inch-thick rounds
2 celery stalks, cut into 1-inch pieces
2 large onions, cut in half, one half stuck with 2 cloves
2 sprigs fresh thyme, or ½ tsp. dried thyme leaves
1 or 2 bay leaves
10 to 15 parsley stems
5 black peppercorns

Put the chicken trimmings and bones into a heavy stockpot; pour in enough water to cover them by about 2 inches. Bring the liquid to a boil over medium heat, skimming off the scum that rises to the surface. Lower the heat and simmer the liquid for 10 minutes, skimming and adding a little cold water to help precipitate the scum.

Add the carrots, celery, onions, thyme, bay leaves, parsley, and peppercorns, and submerge them in the liquid. If necessary, pour in enough additional water to cover the contents of the pot. Simmer the stock for two to three hours, skimming as necessary to remove the scum.

Strain the stock and allow it to stand until tepid, then refrigerate it overnight or freeze it long enough for the fat to congeal. Spoon off and discard the layer of fat.

Tightly covered and refrigerated, the stock may safely be kept for three to four days. Stored in small, tightly covered freezer containers and frozen, the stock may be kept for as long as six months.

EDITOR'S NOTE: *The chicken gizzard and heart may be added to the stock. Wings and necks—rich in natural gelatin—produce a particularly gelatinous stock, ideal for sauces and jellied dishes.*

Vegetable Stock

Makes about 2 quarts
Working time: about 25 minutes
Total time: about 1 hour and 30 minutes

4 celery stalks with leaves, cut into 1-inch pieces
4 carrots, peeled and cut into 1-inch pieces
4 large onions, coarsely chopped
3 large broccoli stems, coarsely chopped (optional)
1 medium turnip, peeled and cut into ½-inch cubes
6 garlic cloves, crushed
¼ cup parsley leaves and stems, coarsely chopped
10 black peppercorns
4 sprigs fresh thyme, or 1 tsp. dried thyme leaves
2 bay leaves

Put the celery, carrots, onions, broccoli, if you are using it, turnip, garlic, parsley, and peppercorns into a heavy stockpot. Pour in enough cold water to cover the contents by about 2 inches. Bring the liquid to a boil over medium heat, skimming off any scum that rises to the surface. When the liquid reaches a boil, stir in the thyme and the bay leaves. Lower the heat, cover the pot, leaving the lid slightly ajar, and let the stock simmer undisturbed for one hour.

Strain the stock into a large bowl, pressing down lightly on the vegetables to extract all their liquid. Discard the vegetables. Allow the stock to stand until it is tepid, then refrigerate or freeze it.

Tightly covered and refrigerated, the vegetable stock may safely be kept for five to six days. Stored in small, tightly covered freezer containers and frozen, the stock may be kept for as long as six months.

Fish Stock

Makes about 2 quarts
Working time: about 15 minutes
Total time: about 40 minutes

2 lb. lean-fish bones, fins and tails discarded, the bones rinsed thoroughly and cut into large pieces
2 onions, thinly sliced
2 celery stalks, chopped
1 carrot, peeled and thinly sliced
2 cups dry white wine
2 tbsp. fresh lemon juice
1 leek, trimmed, split, cleaned (technique, page 127), and sliced (optional)
3 garlic cloves crushed (optional)
10 parsley stems
3 sprigs fresh thyme, or 1 tsp. dried thyme leaves
1 bay leaf
5 black peppercorns, cracked

Put the fish bones, onions, celery, carrot, wine, lemon juice, 2 quarts of cold water, and the leek and garlic, if you are using them, into a large, nonreactive stockpot. Bring the liquid to a boil over medium heat, then lower the heat to maintain a simmer. Skim off all the scum that rises to the surface.

Add the parsley, thyme, bay leaf, and peppercorns, and gently simmer the stock for 20 minutes more.

Strain the stock; allow the solids to drain thoroughly before discarding them. Let the stock stand until it is tepid, then refrigerate or freeze it.

Tightly covered and refrigerated, the stock may safely be kept for three days. Stored in small, tightly covered freezer containers and frozen, the stock may be kept for as long as two months.

EDITOR'S NOTE: *Because the bones from oilier fish produce a strong flavor, be sure to use the bones from lean fish only. Sole, flounder, turbot, and other flatfish are best. Do not include the fish skin; it could discolor the stock.*

Glossary

Acidulated water: a dilute solution of lemon juice in water, used to keep certain vegetables from discoloring after they are peeled.

Balsamic vinegar: a mild, intensely fragrant wine-based vinegar made in northern Italy; it is traditionally aged in wooden casks.

Basil: a leafy herb with a strong, spicy aroma when fresh, often used in Italian cooking. Covered with olive oil and refrigerated in a tightly sealed container, fresh basil leaves may be kept for up to six months.

Belgian endive: a small, cigar-shaped vegetable, composed of many tightly wrapped white to pale yellow leaves.

Blanch: to partially cook food by immersing it briefly in boiling water.

Bresaola: whole beef fillet that has been cured in salt and air-dried. It is a specialty of the Lombardy region of Italy and is sold in wafer-thin slices in delicatessens.

Brochette: the French name for a skewer; also refers to skewered and broiled or grilled meat, fish, or vegetables.

Buckwheat flour: a strongly flavored flour made from roasted buckwheat seeds.

Bulgur: whole-wheat kernels that have been steamed, dried, and cracked.

Calorie (or kilocalorie): a precise measure of the energy food supplies when it is broken down for use in the body.

Canelle knife: a kitchen utensil used to create small grooves in vegetables for decorative purposes.

Cardamom: the bittersweet, aromatic dried seeds or whole pods of a plant in the ginger family; often used in curries.

Cayenne pepper: a fiery powder ground from the seeds and pods of various hot red peppers; used in small amounts to heighten other flavors.

Celeriac (also called celery root): the knobby, tuberous root of a plant in the celery family.

Chili peppers: a variety of hot or mild red or green peppers. Fresh or dried, most chili peppers contain volatile oils that can irritate the skin and eyes; they must be handled with extreme care (cautionary note, page 18).

Chili powder: a peppery red powder made from dried ground chili peppers. It is available in various strengths from mild to hot.

Cholesterol: a waxlike substance manufactured in the human body and also found in foods of animal origin. Although a certain amount of cholesterol is necessary for proper body functioning, an excess can accumulate in the arteries, contributing to heart disease. See also Monounsaturated fat; Polyunsaturated fat; Saturated fat.

Cilantro (also called fresh coriander or Chinese parsley): the fresh leaves of the coriander plant; it imparts a lemony, slightly bitter flavor to many Latin American, Indian, and Asian dishes.

Cloud-ear mushrooms (also called tree ears, tree fungus, mo-er, and wood ears): silver-edged, flavorless lichen used primarily for their crunchy texture and dark color. Sold dried, the mushrooms should be soaked in hot water for 20 minutes before they are used.

Coriander: an herb whose earthy-tasting seeds are often used as an ingredient in curries.

Cumin: the aromatic seeds of a plant related to caraway. Raw, the seeds add a slightly bitter flavor to curry and chili powders; toasted, they have a nutty taste.

Daikon radish: a long, white Japanese radish.

Dark sesame oil: a dark seasoning oil, high in polyunsaturated fats, made from toasted sesame seeds. Because the oil has a relatively low smoking point, it is rarely heated. Dark sesame oil should not be confused or replaced with lighter sesame cooking oils.

Debeard: to remove the fibrous threads from a mussel. These threads, called the beard, are produced by the mussel to attach itself to stationary objects.

Devein: to remove the intestinal vein that runs along the outer curve of a shrimp. To devein a shrimp, peel it first, then make a shallow cut along the line of the vein and scrape out the vein with the tip of a knife.

Escarole: a broad-leafed green with a pleasantly bitter flavor, best used with sweeter greens.

Fennel (also called anise, *finocchio,* and Florence fennel): a vegetable with feathery green tops and a thick, white bulbous stalk. It has a milky, licorice flavor and can be eaten raw or cooked.

Feta cheese: a salty Greek and Middle Eastern cheese made from goat's or sheep's milk. The curds are ripened in their own salted whey.

Five-spice powder: a pungent blend of ground Sichuan pepper, star anise, cassia, cloves, and fennel seeds. It is available in Asian food shops.

Garam masala: an aromatic mixture of ground spices used in Indian cooking. It usually contains coriander, cumin, cloves, ginger, and cinnamon. It is available in Asian shops and some supermarkets.

Ginger: the spicy, buff-colored rhizome, or rootlike stem, of the ginger plant, used as a seasoning either fresh or dried and powdered. Dried ginger makes a poor substitute for fresh ginger.

Goat cheese: a pungent soft cheese made with goat's milk.

Goujonettes: small fish or strips of fish that have been coated with crumbs before cooking.

Gratin: a baked dish with a crunchy topping of breadcrumbs or grated cheese browned in the oven or under the broiler.

Jerusalem artichoke (also called sunchoke): neither an artichoke nor from Jerusalem, this American vegetable is the tuberous root of a member of the sunflower family. In texture, color, and flavor, it resembles the water chestnut. "Jerusalem" may derive from the Italian word *girasole,* meaning a plant whose flowers turn toward the sun.

Julienne: the French term for vegetables or other food cut into matchstick-size strips.

Kumquat: a fruit that resembles a tiny orange, with a thin and edible peel. Kumquats are ofted used to garnish savory dishes.

Lamb's lettuce (also called corn salad or mâche): soft tongue-shaped leaves with a nutlike sweetness and underlying astringency.

Lemon grass (citronella): a long, woody, lemon-flavored stalk that is shaped like a scallion. Lemon grass is available in Asian shops. To store, refrigerate in plastic wrap for up to two weeks; lemon grass may also be frozen for storage.

Madeira: a fortified wine, often used in cooking, that is produced on the island of Madeira. There are four classes of Madeira, ranging from sweet to dry in flavor and brown to gold in color.

Marinade: a mixture of aromatic ingredients in which meat or vegetables are allowed to stand before cooking to enrich their flavor. Some marinades will tenderize meat, but they do not penetrate deeply.

Marjoram: sweet marjoram and its heartier relative pot marjoram are aromatic herbs, related to oregano but milder in flavor.

Marsala: a fortified dessert wine named after the region of Sicily where it originated. Most varieties are sweet in flavor and brown in color.

Mirin: a sweet Japanese cooking wine made from rice. If mirin is unavailable, substitute white wine or sake mixed with an equal amount of sugar.

Monounsaturated fat: one of the three types of fats found in foods. Monounsaturated fats are believed not to raise the level of cholesterol in the blood. Some evidence indicates that oils high in monounsaturated fats—olive oil, for example—may even lower the blood-cholesterol level.

Nappa cabbage (also called Chinese cabbage): an elongated cabbage resembling Romaine lettuce, with long broad ribs and crinkled, light green to white leaves.

Nonreactive pan: a cooking vessel whose surface does not chemically react with food. Materials used include stainless steel, enamel, glass, and some alloys. Untreated cast iron and aluminium may react with acids, producing discoloration or a peculiar taste.

Nori: paperlike dark green or black sheets of dried seaweed, often used in Japanese cuisine as flavoring or as wrappers for rice and vegetables.

Oakleaf lettuce: a delicate red-leafed lettuce.

Olive oil: any of various grades of oil extracted from olives. Extra-virgin olive oil has a full, fruity flavor and very low acidity. Virgin olive oil is lighter in flavor and slightly higher in acidity. Pure olive oil, a processed blend of olive oils, has the lightest taste and highest acidity. For salad dressings, virgin and extra-virgin olive oils are preferred. Store in a cool, dark place.

Pesto: a smooth paste made by pounding basil, garlic, pine nuts, and salt with olive oil. In Italian, *pesto* simply means "pounded."

Phyllo: a paper-thin flour-and-water pastry popular in Greece and the Middle East. It can be bought fresh or frozen from delicatessens and shops specializing in Middle Eastern food.

Pine nuts (also called *pignoli*): seeds from the cone of the stone pine, a tree native to the Mediter-ranean. Pine nuts are used in pesto and other sauces; their buttery flavor can be heightened by light toasting.

Plantain: a green-skinned banana-like fruit, popular in West Indian and African cuisine. It must be cooked before it is eaten.

Poach: to cook food in barely simmering liquid as a means of preserving moisture and adding flavor.

Polyunsaturated fat: one of the three types of fat found in foods. Polyunsaturated fats, which exist in abundance in such vegetable oils as safflower, sunflower, corn, and soybean, lower the level of cholesterol in the blood.

Porcini (also called cepes): wild mushrooms with a pungent, earthy flavor that survives drying or long cooking. Dried porcini should be soaked in hot water for 20 minutes before they are used.

Prosciutto: an uncooked, dry-cured, and slightly salty Italian ham, sliced paper thin.

Quenelle: a purée of meat or fish, bound with egg whites and cream, then shaped into ovals and poached. Low-fat quenelles can be made by using yogurt in place of the cream.

Radicchio: a purplish red Italian chicory with a chewy texture and slightly bitter taste.

Recommended Dietary Allowance (RDA): the average daily amount of an essential nutrient as recommended for groups of healthy people by the National Research Council.

Red-leaf lettuce: a red-tinged, frilly lettuce.

Reduce: to boil down a liquid in order to concentrate its flavor and thicken its consistency.

Refresh: to rinse a briefly cooked vegetable under cold water to arrest its cooking and set its color.

Rice-paper wrappers: wafer-thin, translucent disks made of rice and water; they become supple after a few seconds when dipped in cold water. They are sold in Oriental shops.

Rice vinegar: a mild, fragrant vinegar that is less assertive than cider vinegar or distilled white vinegar. It is available in dark, light, seasoned, and sweetened varieties; Japanese rice vinegar generally is milder than the Chinese version.

Ricotta cheese: soft, mild, white Italian cheese, made from cow's or sheep's milk. Full-fat ricotta has a fat content of 20 to 30 percent, but the low-fat ricotta used in this book has a fat content of only about 8 percent.

Rock shrimp (also called Dublin Bay prawns, langoustine, or lobsterettes): a large crustacean, found in the Atlantic, Mediterranean, and Adriatic, that looks like a small lobster. The meat, mainly in the tail, is firm and sweet.

Roe: refers primarily to fish eggs, but edible roe is also found in scallops, crabs, and lobsters.

Safflower oil: the vegetable oil that contains the highest proportion of polyunsaturated fats.

Saffron: the dried, yellowish red stigmas (or threads) of the saffron crocus, which yield a powerful yellow color as well as a pungent flavor. Powdered saffron may be substituted for threads but has less flavor.

Sake: Japanese rice wine. If sake is not available, dry sherry may be substituted.

Sambal oelek: an Indonesian sauce made from chili peppers. Available in Asian shops, sambal oelek makes an excellent substitute for fresh or dried chili peppers.

Saturated fat: one of the three types of fat present in foods. Found in abundance in animal products and in coconut and palm oils, saturated fats raise the level of cholesterol in the blood. Because high blood-cholesterol levels may contribute to heart disease, saturated-fat consumption should be restricted to less than 10 percent of the calories provided by the daily diet.

Sauté: to cook a food quickly in a small amount of oil or butter over high heat, stirring or tossing the food often to keep it from burning or sticking.

Savoy cabbage: a variety of head cabbage with a mild flavor and crisp, crinkly leaves.

Sesame oil: see Dark sesame oil.

Sesame seeds: small, nutty-tasting seeds used frequently, either raw or roasted, in Middle Eastern and Indian cuisine.

Sherry vinegar: a full-bodied vinegar made from sherry; it has a sweet aftertaste.

Shiitake mushroom: a variety of mushroom, originally grown only in Japan, available fresh or dried. The dried form should be soaked in hot water for 20 minutes and stemmed before use.

Simmer: to cook a liquid just below its boiling point so that the liquid's surface barely trembles.

Skim milk: milk from which almost all the fat has been removed.

Sodium: a nutrient essential to maintaining the proper balance of fluids in the blood. In most diets, a major source of the element is table salt, made up of 40 percent sodium. Excess sodium may cause high blood pressure, a contributor to heart disease. One teaspoon of salt, with 2,132 milligrams of sodium, contains almost two-thirds of the maximum "safe and adequate" daily intake recommended by the National Research Council.

Soy sauce: a savory, salty brown liquid made from fermented soybeans and available in both light and dark versions. One tablespoon of ordinary soy sauce contains 1,030 milligrams of sodium; lower-sodium variations, such as naturally fermented shoyu, may contain only half that amount. See also Tamari.

Steam: to cover food and cook it in the steam created by a boiling liquid. Steaming vegetables preserves the vitamins and flavors that are ordinarily lost in boiling.

Stir-fry: to cook thin slices of vegetables, fish, or meat over high heat in a small amount of oil, stirring constantly to ensure even cooking in a short time. The traditional cooking vessel is a wok; a heavy-bottomed frying pan may also be used.

Sushi rice: short-grained rice that is moist, firm, and sticky when cooked. It is available in Oriental food shops.

Tahini (also called sesame paste): a nutty-tasting paste made from ground sesame seeds that are usually roasted.

Tamari: a dark, strong-flavored soy sauce, sometimes described as unfermented or raw soy because of its shorter brewing period.

Tamarind (also called Indian date): the pulp surrounding the seeds of the tamarind plant, yielding a juice considerably more sour than lemon juice. Grown and used throughout Asia, tamarind is available fresh in pod form, in bricks, or as a concentrate.

Tarragon: a strong herb with a sweet anise taste. Because heat intensifies tarragon's flavor, cooked dishes require smaller amounts.

Thyme: a versatile herb with a zesty, slightly fruity flavor and a strong aroma.

Total fat: an individual's daily intake of poly-unsaturated, monounsaturated, and saturated fats. Nutritionists recommend that fats constitute no more than 30 percent of a person's total calorie intake. The term as used in the nutrient analyses in this book refers to all the sources of fat in a recipe.

Turmeric: a yellow spice from a plant related to ginger, used as a coloring agent and occasionally as a substitute for saffron. Turmeric has a musty odor and a slightly bitter flavor.

Wakame: a seaweed used in Japanese cooking. Bought in dried form, it must be soaked in tepid water for 20 minutes before use.

Wasabi: a Japanese horseradish, usually sold in powdered form. The powder is mixed with water to form a fiery green paste, which is then served with sushi or noodles.

Wild rice: the seed of a water grass native to the Great Lakes region of the United States. It is appreciated for its nutty flavor and chewy texture.

Won-ton wrapper: a thin dough wrapper, about 3½ inches square, made of wheat flour and egg and used to encase spicy fillings of meat, fish, or vegetables.

Index

Picture Credits

Credits for the illustrations from left to right are separated by semicolons; credits from top to bottom are sepatated by dashes.

Cover: Chris Knaggs. 4: James Murphy—Chris Knaggs; John Elliott. 5: James Murphy—Chris Knaggs. 6: Chris Knaggs. 10: Ian O'Leary. 12, 13: Martin Brigdale. 14-17: Philip Modica. 18-21: James Murphy. 22: Philip Modica; Taran Z. Photography. 23: Chris Knaggs. 24: Simon Butcher. 25: James Murphy—Chris Knaggs. 27, 28: John Elliott. 29: James Murphy. 30, 31: John Elliott. 32: Chris Knaggs. 33: John Elliott. 34: Jan Baldwin. 35: James Murphy. 36-39: Chris Knaggs. 40: John Elliott. 41: Andrew Whittuck. 42-45: John Elliott. 46: Philip Modica. 47, 48: John Elliott. 49: Chris Knaggs. 50-53: Jan Baldwin. 54-56: Chris Knaggs. 57: Andrew Whittuck. 58: Chris Knaggs. 59: Philip Modica. 60: Jan Baldwin. 61: Chris Knaggs. 62: Jan Baldwin. 63, 64: John Elliott. 65: Chris Knaggs. 66: Jan Baldwin—John Elliott. 67: Jan Baldwin. 68, 69: John Elliott. 70: Philip Modica. 71: Chris Knaggs. 72: Andrew Whittuck. 73: Philip Modica. 74, 75: John Elliott. 76: John Elliott; Taran Z. Photography (2). 77: John Elliott. 78: Jan Baldwin. 79: Chris Knaggs. 80: John Elliott. 81: Chris Knaggs. 82: Philip Modica. 83: David Johnson. 84: John Elliott. 85: Andrew Whittuck. 86-88: Chris Knaggs. 89: John Elliott. 90: Andrew Whittuck. 91: Chris Knaggs. 92-94: John Elliott. 95: Jan Baldwin. 96: Andrew Whittuck. 97: Philip Modica. 98: John Elliott—Andrew Whittuck. 99: Philip Modica. 100, 101: Jan Baldwin. 102, 103: Chris Knaggs. 104, 105: James Murphy. 106: John Elliott. 107-111: James Murphy. 112, 113: Chris Knaggs. 114: James Murphy. 115, 116: Chris Knaggs. 117: James Murphy. 118: John Elliott. 119: James Murphy. 120: James Murphy—Renée Comet. 121, 122: Chris Knaggs. 123: Martin Brigdale. 124: Jan Baldwin. 125: Chris Knaggs. 126: John Elliott. 127: Chris Knaggs—Taran Z. Photography. 128-138: John Elliott.

Props: The editors wish to thank the following outlets and manufacturers; all are based in London unless otherwise stated. 4: top: china, Fortnum & Mason. 5: plate, Hutschenreuther (U.K.) Ltd.; fork, Mappin & Webb Silversmiths—plate, Villeroy & Boch. 6: china, Hutschenreuther (U.K.) Ltd. 14: plate, Rosenthal (London) Ltd.—bowl, Royal Copenhagen Porcelain and Georg Jensen Silversmiths Ltd. 15: plate, Hutschenreuther (U.K.) Ltd. 16: top: bowl, Rosenthal (London) Ltd. 17: plate, Rosenthal (London) Ltd. 18: bowl, Royal Copenhagen Porcelain and Georg Jensen Silversmiths Ltd. 19: china, Fortnum & Mason. 23: china, Fortnum & Mason; lace cloth, Laura Ashley. 25: bottom: platter, Royal Worcester, Worcester. 30: plates, Hutschenreuther (U.K.) Ltd. 33: plate, Rosenthal (London) Ltd.; Formica, Newcastle, Tyne and Wear. 34: tablecloth, Osborne & Little plc. 36: tablecloth, Ewart Liddell. 37: china, Hutschenreuther (U.K.) Ltd. 39: plate, Rosenthal (London) Ltd. 42: plates, The Mid Wales Development Centre. 46: marble, W. E. Grant & Co. (Marble) Ltd. 48: pottery, Winchcombe Pottery, The Craftsmen Potters Shop. 50: silver, Mappin & Webb Silversmiths; glasses, Kilkenny. 54, 55: pottery, Tony Gant, The Craftsmen Potters Shop. 56: top: napkin, Kilkenny. 58: carpet and plates, Persian Rugs Gallery Ltd. 59: plates, Spode, Worcester. 66: top: pottery, Clive Bowen, The Craftsmen Potters Shop. 67: china, Hutschenreuther (U.K.) Ltd. 75: plate, Rosenthal (London) Ltd. 77: lace cloth, Laura Ashley. 80: plate, Royal Worcester, Worcester; candelabra, Mappin & Webb Silversmiths. 83: plate, Rosenthal. 85: plate, Hutschenreuther (U.K.) Ltd. 87: china, Fortnum & Mason. 90: platter, Royal Worcester, Worcester. 98: pottery, Winchcombe Pottery, The Craftsmen Potters Shop. 100: plate, Royal Worcester, Worcester. 104: china, Spode, Worcester; flatware, Mappin & Webb Silversmiths. 105: china, Hutschenreuther (U.K.) Ltd.; spoon, Mappin & Webb Silversmiths. 109: china, Hutschenreuther (U.K.) Ltd.; fork, Mappin & Webb Silversmiths; cloth, Ewart Liddell. 110, 111: plates, Royal Worcester, Worcester; plate, Hutschenreuther (U.K.) Ltd. 118: flatware, Mappin & Webb Silversmiths. 121: plate, Villeroy & Boch. 123: napkin, Kilkenny. 126: plate, Royal Worcester, Worcester; napkin, Ewart Liddell. 127: top: plate, Micky Doherty, The Craftsmen Potters Shop. 128: marble, W. E. Grant & Co. (Marble) Ltd. 134: china, Chinacraft Ltd. 135: plates, Villeroy & Boch. 138: flour jar, Andrew and Jane Young, The Craftsmen Potters Shop.

Acknowledgments

The editors of Time-Life Books are particularly indebted to the following people and institutions: Paul van Biene, London; René Bloom, London; Maureen Burrows, London; Stuart Cullen, London; Jonathan Driver, London; Irena Hoare, London; Molly Hodgson, Richmond, Yorkshire; Lawleys, London; Line of Scandinavia, London; Next Interiors, London; Christine Noble, London; Oneida, London; Perstorp Warerite Ltd., London; Katherine Reeve, London; Sharp Electronics (U.K.) Ltd., London; Jane Stevenson, London; Toshiba (U.K.) Ltd., London.

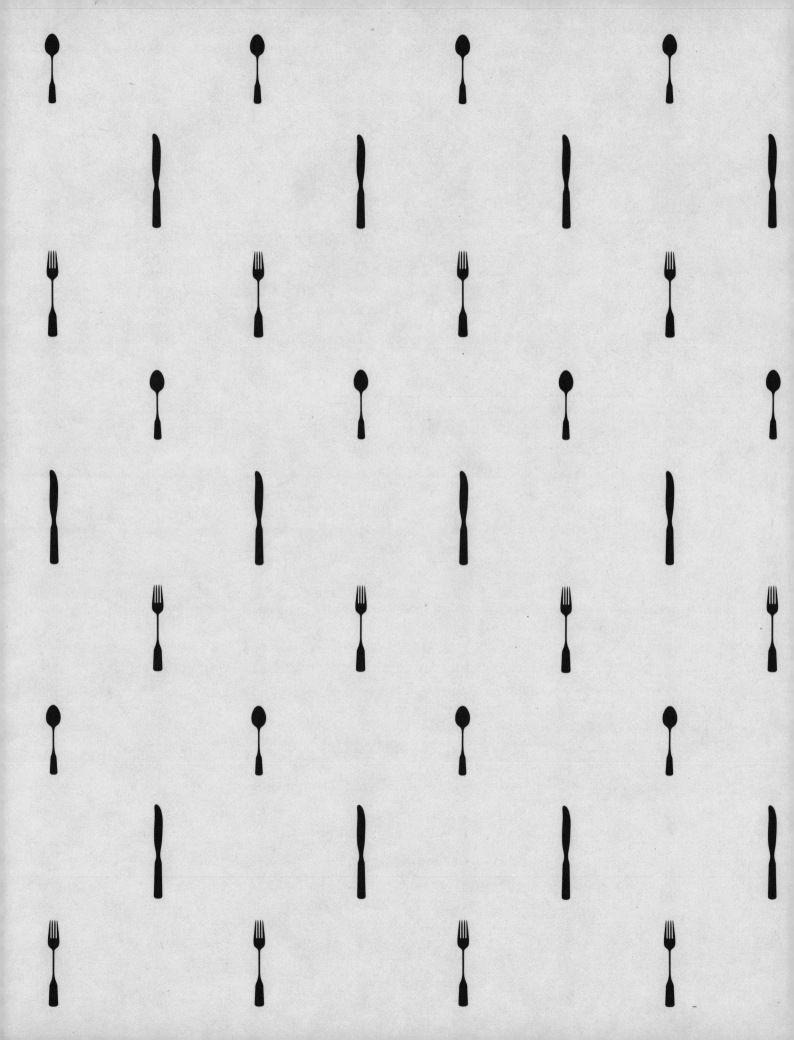